GRAND COVE

GRAND COVE

BY

Jim Wood

1stBooks – rev. 5/22/01

Table of Contents

Chapter 1   The Plan

The six-story red-brick City Hall building stood alone on the grassy esplanade between Grand Cove Bay and Grand Cove Boulevard. It was the only building allowed along the bayfront. The entrance was off of Grand Cove Boulevard that ran along the western side of the building.

The divided boulevard was lined with palm trees whose fronds rustled from the constant breeze that blew in from the bay. The rear of the building was to the east, backing up to the seawall and Grand Cove Bay.

From the distance it was hard to tell for sure what the appendage was that jutted out toward the bay from the top floor of Grand Cove City Hall. It wasn't visible from the front of the building but if you walked toward the bayside and looked up at the thing you could see it was a balcony, made of dark steel. It was totally out of character with the motif of the handsome old structure that had withstood hard times and strong winds.

It was right at five o'clock on Friday afternoon and the city was beginning to wind down for the day and the weekend. Vehicles moved up and down Grand Cove Boulevard, traveling in herds as they stopped and started at the traffic lights.

Mayor Roger Goodenough had retired to the balcony to contemplate the coming evening and those leading up to it. The balcony was larger than it appeared to be from the ground. High protective railings had been erected so some silly bastard wouldn't fall off - or jump off - after he had visited with the mayor and had too much scotch and bay water (SBW).

Goodenough walked to the wet bar, selected a large glass, dropped in handful of ice chucks and poured in a strong shot of scotch. He held the glass under a facet and flicked the ebony handle and watched the glass fill with bay water. He took an appreciative sip and eased his six foot two frame into a black metal chair lined with all weather cushions. It and all of the other furniture were bolted to the bottom of the balcony so high winds couldn't shove them around.

The mayor liked his balcony although members of the City Pretty Committee (CPC), headed by one Miss Lolita, had raised holy hell when he had it built, shortly after being elected mayor four months ago. The design hadn't been approved by anyone and almost everyone agreed it was in pretty poor taste. But Goodenough told them and anyone else who inquired, "The hell with it. I paid for it out of my own pocket."

"And," he would add as an afterthought, "I am the goddamn mayor." Rich, too, he could have added, but didn't. He figured everyone knew that. And he needed a place to think. If he was going to realize the goal he and other leaders of Grand Cove had set, he needed his own space and he'd tear the thing down when he left office anyway. Maybe black metal wasn't the best choice, but he never claimed to be perfect - just the mayor and rich at that and not one to take a lot of crap in the first place.

Goodenough took another pull on his drink. He could, he admitted, make a damn good drink and he used bay water. It actually was water from a small artesian spring inland from Grand Cove - the Grand Cove Bay Springs. Limited amounts of the pure water were bottled and sold in grocery stores. Mayor Goodenough kept a large keg of it behind his wet bar on the balcony and some of the upscale bars used it too.

When occasional visitors were sitting on the balcony and having a drink with the mayor they always commented on the taste of the water. Goodenough told them it was pure bay water, unique to Grand Cove. The visitors were impressed.

He glanced out over Grand Cove Bay.

The view from the balcony was beautiful, the water and the sky converging. In the distance a sail boat tacked against the wind. Closer in seagulls swooped around the Grand Cove Marina, where boats were docked, diving occasionally to the water to pluck at something. One stood on the seawall that had been built years ago to protect the city from flooding from the bay, particularly when there was a storm. Grand Cove had weathered several but had been spared for more than a decade. Some old timers said she was due for a hit.

Goodenough allowed himself a rare chuckle as he looked at the seagull standing on the seawall. It stood on one leg, the other tucked under its breast and not visible. More than once he had pointed out a standing seagull to a visitor who was sipping on scotch and bay water, telling them it was a one-legged gull, also unique to Grand Cove. God, people would believe anything.

He took another sip and sighed. The new man would be arriving shortly to accompany him to what could be the most important meeting of his new administration.

Never one to second guess himself, Goodenough thought he hired the best man for the job. If not, he'd kick his ass out in a New York minute, but in the meantime he would give him his head. The new man was hired after a national search by a head hunting firm. His mission was to upsize Grand Cove, which Goodenough and other leaders considered the country's best kept secret - a real pearl set along a slice of the Texas Gulf Coast known as the Coastal Bend. The focus would be on attracting more tourists, conventions and industries.

Grand Cove wasn't completely unknown. There was some activity. Visitors who knew of it would stop over in Grand Cove on their way to the barrier islands to sun bathe, swim or fish. Others came to sail in Grand Cove Bay or just hang out.

They would put themselves up in second rate hotels or in Grand Cove's only resort hotel, the Sons & Pete Hotel that set back a block from the seawall. It was owned and operated by Pete Garcia and his two sons. In explaining the name he would say, "I always put my sons first." Locals referred to it simply as the Sons Hotel.

Now and again a small convention would gather in Grand Cove but because space was limited the city could never go for a medium sized convention, let along a big one. The conventions that did come would meet in the Sons Hotel or the Grand Cove Convention Center, something of a misnomer many thought. The Convention Center was situated a block west of the Sons Hotel, two blocks inland from the bay. With its semicircular, arching roof and low fit to the ground, it squatted more than set and looked more like an enlarged Quonset hut than a convention center. The smaller conventions usually opted for the Sons Hotel which had limited meeting space but a great bar.

There was also a small port where ships picked up grain that was grown in the region or brought in crude oil to be refined in the city's two petrochemical plants. A few prostitutes operated out of motels located on the north side of the port, away from the main city. The motels were popular with merchant seamen who came in with the ships, as well as Grand Covians when they got horny. Jenette and her Port Girls monitored the shipping logs regularly so they would know when a ship was due in port.

******

It had taken several months for the head hunters to find someone to lead the new promotional effort. They reminded Mayor Goodenough that while there were any number of executives qualified to downsize businesses by firing most of the help there weren't a lot of them good at upsizing anything. And on top of that, they told him, competition was fierce among cities, states and even countries for promoters who could bring in a buck.

"I don't give a rat's ass," Goodenough told them. "Find me The Man." After all, he was offering to pay good money. After a lot of deep thinking and retreats, most held on the City Hall balcony, others on the mayor's ranch, it was concluded that what Grand Cove needed for the new position was a real promoter. He would be hired as executive director of the newly created Commission on Tourism, Industry and Conventions (CO-TIC).

Goodenough and a small group of advisors who had created CO-TIC settled on a man named Botsford Botsford, who went by Botch. While CO-TIC was the official acronym, the members soon referred to themselves as the Usual Suspects.

Botch had a good resume, at least as Mayor Goodenough saw it. Among other things Botch had been a circus barker, an ad salesman and most recently, a visionary for what was going to be The Next Cool Thing for a Madison Avenue advertising agency, where he met with limited success. One idea undertaken for a beer company bombed. The concept was to promote a seven-pack of beer accompanied by the slogan, "Drink one on the road and still have six when you get there." It was packaged in such a way that the seventh beer projected lengthwise out from the top of the package and served as a handle until lifted out and drank. Although it never caught on it was popular with some pickup drivers.

Botsford interviewed well. Goodenough was impressed by his assurances that he would develop a plan that couldn't fail. "This town is gonna grow," he said during the interview, a statement delivered with a fast-paced bark. "It's gonna grow. We're gonna promote this puppy outta sight We're gonna spin her."

******

The mayor's thoughts were interrupted by the sliding of the door from his City Hall office to the balcony.

A striking woman stepped softly onto the balcony. Her black hair that was smooth and sheeny hung to her shoulders. Her eyes were a contrasting crystal blue and her skin the color of almonds.

She wore a white, high-necked cover and business suit. She was about five-eight and her legs were muscular, probably from ballet classes she had taken since she was little.

"Mr. Botsford is here," she said. "Will I be going with you to the meeting?"

"Damned right you will, Feather. Gotta have someone there I trust," the mayor replied. "And Feather," he added in an almost fatherly way, "Watch out for this Botch guy. He ain't no Gary Grant but he has a line of bullshit."

"Roger," she chided, a faith blush touching her cheeks.

Feather was Goodenough's dollar-a-year administrative assistant. She had worked in his election campaign and signed on to help out after he got elected. She didn't need to earn any money because the trust fund Goodenough set up years ago took care of her financial needs. She was, after all, his daughter.

Feather was born on Goodenough's ranch, which was situated in a desolate area of South Texas about 100 miles southeast of Grand Cove. It was as much a monument as a ranch, built with money from oil that was discovered on the property years ago. Feather's mother died when she was just a little girl. Goodenough never remarried so it was left to him and the ranch help to raise her, a ranch where everyone was considered family.

Feather grew into a smart, unassuming woman who was sharp as a tack, not to mention a drop dead knockout. And, if need be, she could swear with the best of them, a habit she had picked up, but now largely controlled, from a lifetime with Goodenough.

Goodenough never said much about the early days. The most he ever allowed was simply, "She's my daughter, born on the ranch." She was well attended to and eventually sent to school at the University of Texas at Austin, where she earned a degree in political science.

Goodenough insisted she go to UT-Austin because he wanted her to have the best education possible.

Goodenough spent most of his time now in Grand Cove in his mansion built along the shoreline south of the central city, an area that offered an unblemished view of the bay. The city's other rich people lived there, too, but most could care less if the city grew. In fact, they liked it just like it was - their own little unspoiled paradise.

There were exceptions, such as Benny Slax, who owned the city's only upscale department store - Slax. It was still independently owned and Benny Slax planned to keep it that way. "She may not be a Sax but she's a damned good Slax," he liked to say of his store.

He also knew he needed more business. More tourists and conventioneers would be a boon. He became one of Goodenough's chief lieutenants in the movement to grow the city.

Goodenough and Feather walked back into the mayor's office and into the reception area where Botch was waiting. Botch was not a tall man but neither was he height challenged. He looked to be in the range of five-nine. He was on the chunky side and his round face, almost always in a flush, was accentuated by his thinning hair he wore in a buzz cut.

"All set?" Goodenough asked.

"Let's get it on," Botch replied.

They had earlier gone over the basic format for the meeting, which would be attended by Grand Cove's movers and shakers. Botch would lay the framework for a plan to get the city growing, after Goodenough said a few words.

The mayor initially questioned the rationale of meeting in the cramped Grand Cove Convention Center, but Botch said it would help prove a point.

The three left City Hall and decided to walk to the Convention Center instead of roaring up in the mayor's limousine, an approach that had some appeal to Botch. The sun was arching to the west but there was still plenty of daylight.

"Give it a good shot," the mayor said to Botch as they approached the Convention Center. Judging from the cars parked on the lot there would be a good turnout.

As Goodenough, Feather and Botsford walked under the awing that overhung the entrance to the Convention Center the manager of the center emerged from the double glass doors and strode briskly toward them.

"Bad news, Mayor Goodenough," he said. "The air conditioning system is on the blink again. It's pretty warm in there."

"Crap," the mayor responded.

"That's okay," Botch said. "Helps prove a point."

They entered the building and walked down the corridor to Cove Room 1, where the gathering was taking place. The manager pulled open the door for them and they entered. The room was warm and a rank order permeated it. People were craning their necks sideways and backwards, casting accusing glances.

It was pretty clear someone had just farted.

Feather waved her hand slightly by her nose and took a seat in a metal folding chair near the doorway. Botch and Goodenough walked to a table set up for them at the front of the room, facing the audience of community leaders who sat in metal chairs lined in rows of twenty, some of their butts hanging over the edges of their chairs. Many were sweating.

Goodenough arose from his chair and tapped on a water glass for attention. "We appreciate all of you taking time out of your busy schedules to attend this meeting. I know it's warm because the air conditioner broke down again so I won't keep you too long. But the program we have in store for this grand little city is worth the sweat. Botch Botsford, setting here at my left, will outline it for you.

"Some of you have already met him," the mayor continued. "We'll meet now and again for progress reports. And if any of you have a good idea don't keep it a secret. Let's hear from you. I know I can count on your support." He scanned the audience and nodded toward a man seated in the front row.

"Good to see you M.P. Thanks for coming."

M.P. Booster, chairman of the Greater Grand Cove Chamber of Commerce acknowledged the recognition with a slight wave of his hand. He was a portly man with sagging jowls and held an unlighted cigar in his left hand.

"And Mike I'm glad you could come," he said, addressing Mike Wheelhorse, who owned one of the oil refineries. Wheelhorse, his hair clipped just right and brushed back on the sides, gave a curt nod.

"And we gotta have support from you," Goodenough said, looking at W.E. True, owner and publisher of the Grand Cove Breeze, the city's daily newspaper which always included an ear in the upper left hand corner of Page 1 that said, "If It's In the Breeze, You Know It's True."

He nodded.

"And glad to have you Sassy," the mayor said to the only woman in the audience, Sassy Butte, who ran a curio and lingerie shop - Butte's Hut - that catered to highend locals and visitors. The shop, located next to Benny Slax's department store on Oyster Street, featured sexy underwear, including uplift bras, swim suits, shorts and polished seashells. She had plans to add new lines. Sassy was one of Grand Cove's premier supporters.

She had large breasts that were nearly visible from the low-cut blouses she was fond of wearing and the pushup bra she perfected and marketed under the Sassy Butte brand. "Men like more than a Butte," she proclaimed in her advertisements for the bras.

She had also just completed a new swim suit design for the Grand Covettes, the city's drill and dance team that had been created to help with the promotion of Grand Cove. She had high hopes for marketing this new line, not only for swimsuits but for panties as well. The design included an embroidered, perfectly symmetrical oyster shell whose sides lay invitingly open just below the waist line. GRAND was stitched on the right side and COVE on the left.

Sassy worn a tight fitting skirt that hugged her butte, as she called it. Goodenough liked her as did her business neighbor, Benny Slax. "I'm just trying to make a buck," she had told him many times. "If you're not talking dollars you're not talking American. At least that's the way I look at it."

The mayor removed his gaze from Sassy and turned to Botsford. "It's yours," he said.

Botch pulled a handkerchief from his back pocket and wiped bubbles of sweat from his head. He wadded it into his left hand and leaned forward, his knuckles braced against the table, looking out at the community leaders.

He straightened up, held out his arms and made an upward motion with his hands. "Please rise," he said. There was a shuffling of chairs as the community leaders, about 100 of them, stood.

"Men," he said. "I'm not going to waste your time with a lot of clap-trap. I want to get us on the road to progress. And to mark this first giant step for Grand Cove I say we need a credo, one we can all embrace. After I recite it you join me."

Botch tapped his foot to get a rhythm and recited:

> "The city, the city, the city
> A little bit down a pity
> For awhile we've been sucking hind titty
> But this town is gonna grow."

Now join me," Botsford shouted, his face turning red. They joined in.

> "The city, the city, the city
> A little bit down a pity
> For awhile we've been sucking hind titty
> But this town is gonna grow."

The roar that followed was nearly deafening, not unlike those that used to follow the National Anthem at the start of a Dallas Cowboys football game when the Cowboys were winning. M. P. Booster shot both arms above his head. "Alright. Alright," he shouted and briefly wondered if he was being undignified.

Botch stomped his right foot and barked, "Yes, Yes, Yes."

Sassy was jumping up and down and waving her arms. Her boobs were bouncing and her skirt struggling to stay below her hips. "Go, Grand Cove, Go," she shouted.

There was also that rank odor again, permeating the hot, crowded, smelly room.

Feather sat on the sideline watching it all and wondering, what with all the heat in the room and all the emotion, if the people there were going a little crazy.

After the place had quieted Botch motioned everyone to sit back down.

"I can see some of you are sweating. So am I. This room, this building, is a real piece of crap. How can we expect to get a decent sized convention if we can't offer a decent meeting place," Botch said.

"Where we gonna get it?" Mike Wheelhorse asked from the audience. "The voters have never been real keen on supporting bond issues," he added with a bit of a smirk. Others nodded their agreement.

"They just haven't thought it through," Botch said. "They have to be educated. And I have some ideas we'll talk about later."

"A new convention center will take some time but there are other things we can do right now to get us started on our big three goals — Conventions, Industry and Tourism," Botch continued.

"We'll going to start with the tourist bit, a big promotion to celebrate the first tourist who enters this great little city on the first day of Labor Day Weekend which is just around the corner. T Day we're gonna call it. We'll promote this puppy. Get national publicity." Botch paused to catch his breath and continued.

"We're gonna entertain that lucky person in true Grand Cove style. The Sons Hotel has already agree to provide a suite. And we have some other goodies in store," he continued with a lewd wink. "We're gonna put this little puppy on the map."

"We're gonna also start putting out feelers for a new industry. We gotta have more jobs. We'll have to offer something in return, of course. Every city does. You know, tax breaks, land or something in the way of inducements. I know from the information you folks have provided me that we have a

11

nice pool of workers that an industry can get at right around minimum wage," Botch continued.

There were nods of agreement among the leaders. Feather just sat there watching.

"What else is planned?" a voice from the back of the room asked.

"Many things," Botch replied. "Many things. The program will evolve, a lot of things going on all at one time. We're a work in progress. Benny Slax has some ideas. So does Sassy and M.P. And I've already hired a PR firm that is drawing up a simple little booklet we'll spread around the city and mail to every household pointing out the advantages of the hospitality industry and what our Citizens can do to help. We gotta treat our visitors right and make Grand Covians a part of effort."

"But to get us started on the right foot we're gonna focus first on that First Tourist promotion. And we gotta move fast. We've got just a little more than a month before T Day," Botch continued.

Sassy raised her hand. "If we're going to educate our citizens on how to be nice to tourists maybe they could take some lessons from those ladies who work the docks at the Port of Grand Cove," she said and giggled.

The others in the room snickered and a couple jabbed the person next to them in the ribs.

"You mean screw them," Botch said with a chuckle. "We're certainly going to take their money. That's what tourism is all about."

There were more snickers around the room.

"I know you have to get about your business and you're hot and sweaty so I'll not keep you any longer. But one thing before we go," Botch said. He raised his arms for the audience to rise. They didn't need any prompting as Botsford tapped his foot and brought his right arm down in a chop. They roared in unison.

> "The city the city the city
> A little bit down a pity
> For awhile we've been sucking hind titty
> But this town is gonna grow."

Chapter 2   **The Tourist**

It was hard to get to Grand Cove by accident. You had to want to come. The Grand Cove Municipal Airport didn't have connecting flights to anywhere. You flew into Grand Cove or you didn't. And there were only two highways. The main one, the State Highway, branched off of Interstate 37 from San Antonio, and a lesser traveled one that connected to other roads that meandered along the coastline to and from the Houston area. Traffic from that direction crossed over the Port of Grand Cove on an arched bridge that allowed the ships to enter and leave the port.

The Grand Cove Municipal Airport was situated along the State Highway, about five miles from downtown. For the most part the area on either side of the drive into town was farmland except for an area about a mile out from the north side of the highway, where scavenger gulls could be seen circling the Grand Cove Landfill, as most cities, including Grand Cove, call their garbage dumps. There were also acres of shotgun houses set on small lots, where the city's poor people lived. Botch took notice of the area on his very first drive in from the airport. Not a very pretty sight for visitors, he thought and filed the thought away for another time. His first job was to get people into the city.

Botch said many times that with its limited access people who came to Grand Cove had to want to come. "People don't come here by accident. They gotta wanna come and we're gonna to make'em wanna. Nobody gets here by accident."

He had set in motion the public relations campaign to promote T Day, which would, as planned, take place over the Labor Day Weekend.

The First Tourist would be given a special welcome, a free suite at the Sons Hotel, a tour of the city and a new Sports Utility Vehicle that Botch had wormed out of Slick McSales, who owned the largest auto dealership in the city. There were also some other goodies in store.

Ads were placed in travel magazines and press releases were sent to major dailies across the country with heavy saturation in Texas because Botsford figured most of the traffic would be three-day weekenders. Video tapes were sent to television markets for use as light filler material on a slow news day, videos that showed good looking young women frolicking in Grand Cove Bay.

The Grand Cove Breeze published a series of feature articles about the event and fed stories to the wire services. "We're gonna score big with this First Tourist thing," Botch assured Mayor Goodenough.

****

Police Sgt. Peewee Ratlidge and his squad of officers arrived an hour early to be on the safe side. At the stroke of midnight they would set up a roadblock on the State Highway at the city limits line to await the First Tourist. It had been agreed that the event would be as legitimate as possible and that the best way to identify the First Tourist or group was to catch him or her or them at the city limits line.

Contingency plans had been drawn up to honor whoever showed up but Botch and his people were pulling for a man. Entertaining a family with a bunch of bratty kids wouldn't be much fun and would eliminate one special treat Botch had in store.

Peewee had angled hard to get assigned to the post at the State Highway because it was the most likely place that a tourist suspect would enter first. Logging in the First Tourist could only enhance his reputation as one of the best of Grand Cove's Finest. Peewee stood over six feet tall and had a well developed beer gut that sloped smoothly over his gunbelt. His knuckles were scarred.

He and his officers checked their watches. It was a minute until midnight.

"Block," Peewee commanded and four patrol cars pulled off the shoulders of the highway, the tires of their sedans squealing, and braked with a lurch on the highway. Two portable floodlights were turned on, illuminating the area and the city limits sign. At the last minute Peewee spotted a log laying by the highway and ran to it. With grunts and groans he dragged it onto the highway as a backup. No goddamn way the First Tourist was going to get past his roadblock without being stopped and confirmed.

He and his officers looked down the highway. In the distance they could see approaching headlights. Peewee tensed and a couple of the officers adjusted the revolvers in their holsters. Peewee glanced at his watch. It was a minute after midnight. If the traveler was a Tourist, and whoever it was had better goddamn be a Tourist, then Peewee was sure his team had bagged the winner. He got on his radio and called the dispatcher at Police Headquarters.

"Ratlidge here," he told the dispatcher in a stern voice. "Possible tourist suspect vehicle is approaching. Will provide confirmation after suspect is checked out."

The vehicle eased to a crawl as it approached the roadblock, next to the official city limits sign, which was a big one for a city limits sign.

"Welcome To Grand Cove. The City That Is Gonna Grow," the sign, the size of a billboard, read. The driver seemed to wince as he pulled to a stop. He was in a faded yellow van.

He rolled down the window as Peewee approached and winced again as the glare of the floodlights hit him. "Good evening, sir," Peewee said, leaning into the window. "Here to visit this great little city? I can tell you you're in for a treat."

The man had long yellowish hair and was in need of a shave. He appeared to be twenty something. He was pale. What appeared to be a beatup computer was in the seat next to him.

"Where am I?" he asked.

"You're in Grand Cove, of course," Peewee said. "You down for a little R&R?"

The man seemed puzzled. "Is this Interstate 10 west, the one that leads to California?"

"No sir," Peewee said, beginning to get a little agitated. "This highway leads right to Grand Cove."

"Crap," the man said. "I musta took the wrong turn and got here by accident. I'm on my way to San Jose."

Peewee began to turn red. "Why you," he said and raised a flashlight in his big right hand. "Nobody gets here by accident." The man instinctively began to cower in his seat. "I'm sorry," he said. "I just got lost." Peewee raised his flashlight again.

"Hold on, Peewee," said an officer standing next to him. "Let me talk with him for a minute."

Peewee stepped back and the other officer opened the door and asked the man out. He and his partner led the man to a patrol car and ushered him into the back seat, where they joined him. Peewee remained by the faded yellow van. His practiced ears thought they heard the sounds of night sticks at work.

In no time the officers returned the man, each holding him by his arms to provide support "It was all a mistake, Peewee This guy is a Tourist who wanted to be the first one in Grand Cove for our weekend celebration. Ain't that so, son?" he said to the man who hung limply between the two officers. The man nodded and mumbled, "Me Tourist."

Peewee grinned and strode to his police car. He grabbed a bottle of scotch he kept for emergencies, poured a healthy splash into a paper cup and returned to the Tourist. "Drink this," he said. "You'll feel better and then you're gonna feel a lot better because this little ole city, the one that is gonna grow, has big plans for you. You like pussy?" Peewee asked and playfully jabbed the Tourist in the ribs with his left elbow. The Tourist pulled back in evident pain and then took a long sip from the paper cup and shook his head as it burned its way down his throat. "I'm better," he volunteered.

"Great," Peewee said. He walked to his police car and called the dispatcher again. "Ratlidge here. We've confirmed a Tourist.

We're claiming him as of one minute past midnight. Do you copy?"

"That's a big ten four, sergeant," the dispatcher responded. "He's the first so get'em on down to City Hall. I'll confirm with the Big Shots that you're on your way. And congratulations."

"Roger and out," Peewee said, his voice swelling with excitement. He walked back to the First Tourist. "You're gonna have a great time. Now here's the see-nar- rio. We're gonna stop at a service station and clean you up a little and then we're going in with sirens blaring. There'll be a small welcoming group - the big day is tomorrow. Tonight I'm gonna turn you over to a fellow name of Botch. He'll take it from there but I'd take it kindly if you was to mention that you got a nice reception here at the city limits line."

The tourist finished off the rest of the scotch that was in the paper cup and nodded absently.

******

Near City Hall was a large platform that had been set up for the event. Botch and others were in the welcoming group. Mayor Goodenough had passed on the night welcoming, leaving that part of the ceremony to the hired hands. He would make a major address the following morning.

Off to one side of the platform were a dozen Grand Covettes, each outfitted in one of Sassy Butte's bikinis with their trademark Grand Cove logo. A jazz band contingent from the Grand Cove Municipal Band was also on hand to perform tasteful late-night music.

A sun-bleached blond woman sat daintily in a chair off to one side, her hands folded in the lap of her crisp white dress. Her ample breasts swelled as she breathed.

Botch looked down Grand Cove Boulevard and in the distance he could see flashing lights. He heard the wail of sirens. That would be Peewee with the First Tourist.

Botch turned to the band. "Hit it," he barked. The band struck up a slow jazz piece and the Grand Covettes, standing in a single line began their dance routine, moving slowly and erotically to the beat of the music.

They kicked their legs high, twisted their butts and then leaned way over and shook their boobs, slowly and gently to the beat of the music. Then they drew their hands invitingly over the Grand Cove logo on their bikini bottoms. Sassy, who was standing below the platform with a small crowd of onlookers, marveled at her design but wondered briefly if the bras were a bit too loose even though the girls danced in almost slow motion.

As the band played and the Grand Covettes kicked their legs and twisted their butts and shook their boobs, Peewee arrived. He screeched to a halt and turned off his lights and siren. He opened the passenger side door for the First Tourist and began escorting him to the platform. As they approached a roar went up from the gathered crowd.

"See," Peewee said to the First Tourist. "They're really excited about you." But the excitement was much more libidinous. A huge tit had popped out of the bra of the lead dancer as she bent toward the approaching First Tourist. She hastily stuffed it back in as Peewee and the First Tourist walked up the steps to the platform.

Botch signaled the band and the dancers for quiet and strode toward the end of the platform, his hand extended to the First Tourist, who accepted it with a weak handshake and still a certain puzzled look about him.

"Welcome to Grand Cove," Botch said. "You're in for a treat." He turned to the welcoming committee. "This is a historic day for Grand Cove, the beginning of our efforts that will make the city great."

He held up his right arm. "Let's hear it," he said and hacked down with a sharp motion. The band struck up a lively beat. The welcoming committee and those in the open-air audience began the mantra.

"The city, the city, the city (High kicks from the Covettes)
A little bit down a pity (A shake of their butts)
For awhile we've been sucking hind titty (A shake of their boobs)
But this town is gonna grow." (Arms upstretched to the Grand Cove moon).

With that Botch announced the evening festivities over. He motioned to the sun-bleached blond to come over. She strode to the center of the platform where Botch and the First Tourist were standing, her hips swinging to and fro.

"This is Jenette. She was selected from many, many applicants to be your escort for the night," Botch said to the First Tourist. The man swallowed and seemed to pale again.

"Nice meetin you," she said and flashed a smile.

"We're got a nice suite set up for you at the Sons Hotel," Botch said. "We'll drive over in my limo. Me and some others will be right down the hall from you in case you need anything."

The suite was on the top and tenth floor of the Sons Hotel with a view of Grand Cove Bay through sliding glass doors which could be opened to let in the cool breeze.

*****

The First Tourist flopped himself into a large chair in the suite and stared blankly at the glass doors. Jenette walked into the bedroom. "I'll be right back. Why don't you make us a drink," she said, motioning to the well-stocked wet bar.

She returned shortly, dressed only in a bra and panties that bore Sassy's Grand Cove design, the perfectly symmetrical oyster shells that opened invitingly. She smiled and added, "Before the night's over you can really say you've been in a Grand Cove."

The First Tourist heaved himself out of his chair, walked to the wet bar and poured large shots of scotch into two glasses. He handed her one and took a deep gulp from his.

"We need to talk," he finally managed to say.

"That's cool," she said. "I don't mind a little conversation before sex."

"Why don't you just slip away. You can say later that you got to feeling bad if anybody asks any questions," he said and took a pull on his drink.

Her sunny disposition turned sour. "Slip away?" she snapped. "Are you trying to ruin my reputation. I worked hard to get this assignment."

"No offense," the First Tourist responded. "Its just that I'm tired." He walked back to the bar and poured himself another drink.

"Tired my ass!" Jenette shouted. "Tired my ass! How the hell do you think it'll sound if word got out our most famous visitor wouldn't lay me because he was too goddamn tired." She took a sip of her drink. "Tired my ass."

Her mood changed again and she began to pout. "Don't you like me?" she asked, running her hands over her Grand Cove panties logo.

"You're fine," the First Tourist replied. "It's just that....just that." He struggled for words. He took another sip from his drink. "It's just...it's just that I'm a gay guy." He lurched toward the sliding glass doors. "I need air," he gasped. He slid the doors open and took a deep breath of the cool Grand Cove night air.

Then he collapsed on the floor and began writhing.

Jenette, still clad only in her Grand Cove panties and bra, ran screaming from the suite to the one where Botch was staying and began pounding on the door.

"Grand Cove we've got a problem," she said out loud.

Chapter 3   **Report to the Mayor**

Mayor Goodenough set the meeting for 5 p.m.on his balcony at City Hall. He'd been tied up all day with budget meetings with the city staff. Besides he needed a good stiff drink of scotch and bay water while last night's events were explained.

Botch had called him early in the morning to say the press conference to introduce the First Tourist had been called off and that the First Tourist had left town. He would explain it all later. He'd have some of the Usual Suspects - CO-TIC directors - with him.

The mayor went out onto the balcony a little early so he could have a quiet moment, look at the seagulls and see if there was a thought for the day. He was agitated by it all and the only thing he came up with was a fleeting thought about all the prime real estate occupied by car lots, used and new. My god, they were everywhere. Must be a lot of money in them, he thought, maybe more than oil, since he didn't own a professional sports teams. Or for that matter didn't want to. His focus was Grand Cove.

Shortly, he heard the door from his office to the balcony slide open. Feather walked out and said, Goodenough thought with a touch of sarcasm, "They're here."

"Send'em out," Goodenough said. He grabbed the metal arm rests on his chair and heaved himself out. He walked to the bar and poured himself another drink of scotch and bay water. He was stirring it with his finger as Botch, M.P. Booster, Sassy, Benny Slax and Pete Garcia from the Sons Hotel walked out onto the balcony. The mayor motioned them toward the bar. They could make their own goddamn drinks.

After everyone had claimed a seat and took a sip of their drinks Goodenough walked to the railing of the balcony and leaned back against it, facing the group.

"Well," he said. "Let's get on with the rat killing."

Botch arose from his chair, blushing slightly and sweating even though a breeze was blowing in from the bay. "Mr. Mayor. Let me first say that we have proclaimed the First Tourist project a success. We didn't lose anything and probably gained. From what I've heard today there were quite a few tourists down for the weekend."

Pete Garcia nodded. "The Sons has filled up pretty good although a couple of people staying on the 10th floor said they thought they heard some sort of commotion last night."

"And Sassy and I have had some pretty good drop-in traffic," added Benny Slax, whose department store was next to Sassy's boutique.

"How was it a success?" the mayor asked. "I didn't give a welcoming speech. Not that I give a big rat's ass. But all the shit finally falls back on me. After all, I am the mayor. And where's the TV stories? And what about the big story True and crew had promised us for tomorrow?"

"There will, of course, be a nice story tomorrow," Botch said. " As you know last night's late ceremony was well past deadline so tomorrow was the earliest we could've gotten in anyway. Of course we had to spin it different."

"Keep going," Goodenough said.

"Well," Botch continued and took a pull on his drink, "The First Tourist was welcomed last night and I think it went pretty well. Problem is he got sick later in his hotel suite. Jenette came beating on my door and we called for emergency help, telling them, of course, it was routine so not to come blaring in with their sirens."

"The paramedics couldn't find anything wrong. He was flopping around on the floor so they gave him a shot to quiet him down," Botch continued.

"We drove him, discreetly of course, to the hospital and called in Dr. Well. He's one of us, as you know. He checked that sucker over and over and couldn't find anything wrong with him. Finally, the good doctor did an allergy test on him. You know, one of those quickies where they stick needles in you and read the results right away." Botch paused for a moment to get his breath and take another sip from his drink.

"And?" Goodenough said.

Botch gulped. "Well," he continued, "it turns out this guy is allergic to the air here in Grand Cove."

Sassy shook her head in disbelief. "There's some real screwed up people out there," she said. They all nodded. What absurdity. Allergic to Grand Cove air?

Botch continued, "He finally got to feeling a little better. We drove him out to the city limits where his van was parked, gave him a new Atlas so he don't get lost and a hundred bucks for gas so he could get the hell out of here and on to San Jose. And Peewee...Sgt. Ratlidge...the officer who brought him in had a little talk with him on the way. Grand Cove is nothing but a repressed memory, if anything."

"What about the story that'll be in the paper in the morning?" Goodenough asked.

"I did a couple of TV interviews for tonight's late news and met with a reporter from the Breeze. We said the First Tourist was identified just after midnight and honored appropriately. But that today's activities had to be canceled because the First Tourist was a high ranking federal official who was called back to Washington at the last minute," Botch added, feeling better all the time.

"What was this fed doing here"? the mayor asked.

Botch winked. "We couldn't go into detail but I did leak a little info to the Breeze reporter, on background of course, that there was good reason to believe that he was here on a fact finding mission to check out reports that there was a little city along the Texas Gulf Coast that really had it all together and might become a model for cities asking for federal funds to help improve themselves."

"Is Janette going to keep her fat mouth shut?" Sassy asked matter-of-factly and stared at the group.

"She will or she'll never work the docks of the Port of Grand Cove again," Botch answered. "We'll be OK with her."

Mayor Goodenough took a sip on his drink, found it diluted from the melting ice and walked in long strides over to the bar and freshened it up. He took a deep pull and sighed. "Where are we on the other projects?"

Botch arose from his chair, pulled a notepad from his back pocket and glanced over it.

"We're moving right along," he said. "Some of the long-range things are still being brewed but we have completed the brochure on the importance of being nice to Tourists. It's being mailed to every address in Grand Cove and will also be available at convenience stores, hotels, the library, etc. I believe the citizens will get a good idea of how important Tourists are to the economy."

The mayor nodded. "What else?"

"We're tinkering with some ideas on how to clean up the view visitors get as they drive into the city. That crap near the airport looks bad," Botch said, referring to the garbage dump and slums. "We want our visitors to have a good first impression. That first one is a lasting one."

He turned to M.P. Booster, who sat stuffed into his chair, the cheeks of his butt trying to spill out over the sides. The Greater Grand Cove Chamber of Commerce was coordinating efforts by the Usual Suspects to lure new industry.

"What you got so far?" Botch asked.

Booster worked himself out of his chair, an unlighted cigar in his left hand, and stood and faced the group. "We may be on to something big," he said. "I can't say too much right now cause it's all preliminary. But we've had some feelers about a company that may be interested in building and operating a factory here. It could be real big." He spread his arms open. "Real big."

"Tell me more," the mayor said. Others leaned forward in their chairs, some bouncing lightly on their toes.

Booster, enjoying the moment, said, "Well I can't be much more specific cause I don't have much more detail. You know how these companies work. They won't give their real names until a deal is ready so they use codes. And we sure as hell don't want any other city knowing what we're working on or they'll try to undercut us to land the new factory."

"This city could sure use some new jobs," Wheelhorse said.

"Right," Booster said. "Right. Just let me say we feel pretty good about the prospects and I can say it may well deal with moccasins. When we get a little further along we're going to have to see what we can offer in the way of tax breaks and that sort of thing."

"Moccasins?" the mayor asked and arched an eyebrow.

"Yeah," Booster said. "People do make them and wear them. But that's all I know right now and even that much shouldn't go beyond the confines of this balcony. Word gets out some other city'll eat our lunch."

They all nodded.

Botch was smiling. "That is great, just great, M.P." He turned to the mayor. "Progress is on the way, Mr. Mayor. This city is gonna grow."

He glanced at his notebook and turned to Sassy.

"How's the downtown Christmas parade shaping up?"

Sassy tugged at the ends of her short skirt as she got up from her chair, flashing a nice bit of tanned thigh in the process. Goodenough glanced at the thighs and felt a slight twinge in his groans but quickly put it aside. His focus right now was Grand Cove.

Sassy faced the group. "As you know Botch here has tasked me with the Christmas parade that will run through downtown right after Thanksgiving. We can't wait until too close to Christmas. Most shopping is already done by then."

"I think we'll turn some bucks," she continued. "As of right now we are laying plans for a real live Santa Claus to parachute into the city, landing near Oyster Street with a bag full of candy and things." Oyster Street was near the bayfront, situated just a block west of Grand Cove Boulevard.

"There'll be hot dog and taco and beer stands set up all along the parade route. The Grand Cove Covettes will lead it off, followed by Municipal Band and Santa Claus who'll toss out his candy sticks. Then come the antique cars with our own Mayor Goodenough in the lead one. All of the high school bands from this area will be in on it and there'll be floats from the Grand Cove Junior League and other such groups."

Sassy continued. "Our working theme is, 'Grand Cove. A great place to Spend Christmas.' The emphasis is on Spend."

The mayor took another sip from his glass of scotch and bay water.

"Keep me posted," he said. "You know I got a lot of other crap to worry about but let's keep our priorities in order." He turned to Botch. "When's that tourist brochure going out?"

"Early next week," Botch said. The group began shuffling around, preparing to leave.

"Before we go," Botch said. "Let's keep the faith." He raised his arms to the skies of Grand Cove and hacked down. The group intoned the mantra.

> "The city, the city, the city
> A little bit down a pity
> For awhile we've been sucking hind titty
> But this town is gonna grow."

"Join me," Botch shouted and threw his glass out over the balcony into Grand Cove Bay. All but Feather joined in. She just sat on the sidelines watching it all with a bit of amusement. But Roger had pledged to get the city going and she accepted some of the things that were going on.

Chapter 4   **The Tourist Brochure**

Melody awakened, as she usually did, about 9 in the morning, ready to take on the day. She stretched her naked, feline body and took a deep breath. She patted the pillow next to her while knowing there was no one there. Chip would already be at work, running the data processing center for the Grand Cove National Bank, which her family had founded and owned for years, weathering the storms of bank mergers and takeovers and remaining a local institution. "He's a good guy," she had confided to her group of Best Friends. "But I'm getting tired of his four-inch floppy." They would giggle at her pun.

Melody stretched again, got up and arched her back. She couldn't help but notice the nice slope of her breasts as she glanced into the full-length mirror. "If I were gay I'd go for you," she said to herself and laughed. She slapped her butt lightly and wondered if she would ever have buns of steel. She tried, working out with her Best Friends at the Grand Cove Spa, but didn't worry much about anything. She was a free spirit and a horny one at that and reveled in the privileges that go with being the daughter of the richest banker in town.

Melody padded to the kitchen, put on a pot of coffee and headed for the shower, allowing the warm water to soothe and awaken her more. She toweled her body briskly to get her blood flowing and briefly rubbed the towel across her wet, short-cropped blond hair. She slipped on a robe and went out to get the paper and check the mail, which always came early because of who they were and where they lived - a stone's throw from the mansion of Mayor Goodenough and others who had their homes along Grand Cove Boulevard.

She didn't belt the robe as she walked out, allowing the Grand Cove breeze to blow it open a bit, just enough to flash any neighbors who might be looking. Give'em a cheap thrill, she thought, as she wrapped the right side back around her body and knelt to pick up the paper. She returned to the kitchen and took the coffee pot and a cup out onto the balcony of the two-story house which had a great view of Grand Cove Bay.

She sipped her coffee and thumbed through the mail, which was mostly credit card statements, reflecting her substantial use of them, and advertisements from direct mail organizations, ones that arrived regularly and with no letup in sight.

A slick color brochure slipped from the stack of advertisements. The cover page was titled:

THE IMPORTANCE OF TOURISM TO GRAND COVE
A Citizens Guide on How to Help

She sipped some more coffee and decided to skip breakfast because today she would have lunch with her Best Friends at the Sons Hotel, a monthly ritual devoted to gossip, salad and chardonnay.

She continued scanning the brochure, which explained how every dollar spent by a tourist was respent several times over in Grand Cove, helping local businesses and the economy in general. Tourism, the brochure continued, particularly when coupled with conventions, spurred new development - new hotels and bars and shopping areas. And that led to more job opportunities. What grand futures there could be, she thought, chances to excel as waitpersons and maids who changed sheets, emptied wastecans and disposed of beer cans, liquor bottles and used rubbers.

The Tourist Brochure urged citizens to be helpful, to be nice, to always remember that first impressions are often lasting ones. Help with directions, suggest places to eat and drink and always say, "Yall come back to see us."

There was also a suggestion, one provided by Botch, that if a Grand Covian spotted anyone in the city who seemed lost or disoriented, he/she should approach the person and ask, "Are you a tourist? Can I help? We Are Grand Cove and We're Gonna Grow."

"Remember," the brochure continued, "Every effort helps. And don't he bashful. No Grand Covian Stands So Tall As When He/She Bends to Help a Tourist."

Melody poured another cup of coffee and began opening and closing her thighs as she looked out over Grand Cove Bay. The view and the breeze were intoxicating and made her horny. It was approaching mid-morning. She went back to her bedroom to begin the process of dressing. She would meet her Best Friends noonish.

******

Melody wheeled her Lexus onto the circular entranceway to the Sons Hotel and braked under the awing. She tossed her keys to a valet parking boy and entered the hotel, her round butt swinging behind her well-above-the-knee skirt.

"Ah, Melody," Pete Garcia said as he ushered her into the restaurant, which was on the bayside of the hotel. Large glass windows offered a view of Grand Cove Bay. "Always good to see you." Pete was a hands on hotelier who made it a point to be around to greet the luncheon and dinner crowds. He knew all of the regulars by their first names and what they liked to drink.

"Hi, Pete," she said and pecked him on the cheek. "How's business? Lots of tourists?"

"We're gonna get there," Pete said and signaled to a waitperson who escorted Melody to a corner booth, where three Best Friends were already waiting. In no time at all another waitperson arrived with a glass of chardonnay.

"So, how's it going guys?" Melody asked as she took a sip of her wine. "Met any interesting tourists?"

Best Friend No. 1 rolled her eyes. "I see you've received your brochure."

"Yeah," Melody said. "Kind of corny but something to think about."

"So's how's Chip?" No. 2 asked.

Melody took a big sip from her wine glass, swallowed and rubbed the glass against her bottom lip. "Micro and soft," she laughed.

"You're a mess," No. 3 said. They liked to talk with Melody because she had no inhibitions when discussing her sex life or anyone else's she knew about.

"He's a good guy," Melody said. "But he's more into computers than into me. I'm serious. I sometimes think I intimidate him, maybe turn him off by being too aggressive. But goddamn, I didn't get married to wake up to an empty pillow." She paused for a moment. "Maybe he's getting it somewhere else."

"You're a mess," No. 3 said again, wishing she could be so open.

A waitperson arrived with four Sons Salads, the luncheon speciality the hotel offered for those who liked to sip wine and pick at fresh veggie salads with crab meat. He also brought four more glasses of chardonnay.

As they picked at their salads Melody scanned the place. The usual luncheon crowd was arriving and a few people were sitting at the bar, which was shaped in a vee with seating on both sides. The apex touched the glass windows that overlooked the bay. With such slanted seating everyone at the bar had a grand view of the water and the sky. Pete Garcia believed the view itself justified the hefty prices he charged. It was a nice place to sit and have a few.

Melody continued to scan the room. Her eyes fell on a man sitting at the bar on a stool at the end of the outer slant. He appeared to be eying their booth. He was big and muscular and wore a tee-shirt that outlined his chest and abs. She saw him motion to the bartender.

Shortly a waitperson arrived at their table with four more glasses of wine. "Compliments of the gentleman at the bar," the waitperson said as he placed the drinks around the booth.

Melody finished off her remaining glass and began on the one sent by the stranger at the bar. She was feeling a little light headed from the lack of food - save the picking at the salad - and generous consumptions of white wine.

She leaned over to her Best Friends and asked, "Do you think he's a Tourist?"

"Could well be," No. 1 said. "Haven't seen him around. And he is a hunk. Why don't you find out."

Melody swilled down the rest of her drink. She signaled to a waitperson. "Get me another and send it to the bar and get him whatever he's drinking." She nodded toward the stranger.

Melody walked a little unevenly toward the stranger at the bar and sat herself beside him. "Thanks for the drink," she said. "I'm Melody. Are you a Tourist?"

"Yes," the man said as the bartender sat down another glass of wine for Melody and a double scotch and bay water for the man. "I like your little town here," he said. "Who came up with the idea of bay water and scotch?"

Melody rubbed her wine glass against her bottom lip. "Think it was something our mayor - Mayor Roger Goodenough - started, or at least made popular. Other places picked up on the idea. The Sons here serves it regularly."

Melody took a big swig from her wine glass. "We're little but we're gonna grow. That's the word. Where you from? We're interested in Tourists, you know. At least that's our party line."

"I must say you're well informed about Grand Cove," the stranger said. "I'm just down from Houston for a little deep sea fishing," he added. " Going out tomorrow and take a boat out into the Gulf and see what I can catch."

He paused for a moment and took another sip of his drink. "And believe me, I've caught a lot of things."

Recalling the Tourist Brochure, Melody asked, "Is there anything I can do to help? We want you to feel right at home. Part of our job is to spread goodwill."

The stranger smiled and let his knee brush her's. He took a sip from his drink and turned to face her. "Melody," he said. "Such a pretty name. Can I be open with you?"

"Yes," Melody said, feeling a surge of the god of sex permeate her body. She shuddered. "You can be open and so will I."

"I'm not much on words, but I sure wish you'd show me the bayfront." he said. "I'm staying here at the hotel."

"Sit still for a minute," she said and walked back to the booth where her Best Friends were watching with bemusement and envy. "I'll be right back," she told them. "I'm gonna show this Tourist guy the bayfront."

"We'll be here," No. 3 said. "We'll wait for a report. You really are a mess."

******

In about an hour Melody returned to the booth, her face still slightly flushed but with a smile. Her hair appeared to be wet, perhaps from a shower.

"So did he like the bayfront?" No. 3 asked. She was tipsy by now.

"He said he loved it," Melody said. "He loved the way we Grand Covians spread goodwill."

"You're a mess," No. 3 said again. "I hope you used a rubber."

******

A few days later Melody was sitting on the balcony at her home, sipping on coffee and worried. She had experienced a burning sensation the day before as she took a pee. Sometimes flippant but never one to mess with her well being she had gone to see her gynecologist.

She remembered well the words of Dr. Clitopatria and knew her to be an open and honest person if a little bit blunt. "Melody," she had told her with her patented bluntness, "You've got the clap."

What awesome words! You've got the clap! How could that be? The words resounded around the room. She was a member of the Grand Cove Junior League, a former debutante and one who didn't screw around too much and even then she was careful. Then she recalled the comment of Best Friend No. 3. Oh, God, how she recalled it. "I hope you used a rubber!"

She hadn't. Swept up as she was under the influence of good chardonnay, a horny feeling and the sweep of wind blowing through her legs as she walked with the stranger to his room, she hadn't even thought about a precaution. He seemed so nice, the lousy bastard. If he ever sets foot in Grand Cove again and I learn about it, I'll rip his goddamn balls out. Rip'em right out, she said to herself.

Dr. Clitopatria gave her a shot and a prescription for some powerful antibiotics which the prescription said were for a sinus infection.

"You'll be OK in a few days," the good doctor told her. "But if you've been screwing Chip you've got a problem. He needs to know."

"Have I got a problem? For the last few days he's been screwing my brains out. He's never been like this before," Melody confided.

"Then you best tell him," Dr. Clitopatria said. "If you've got it then he's got it."

And as a parting word she said, "Melody, you've got to learn to keep it zipped up."

******

She had managed a fitful nap but was sitting on the balcony when Chip got home that afternoon. She had fortified herself with chardonnay and was prepared to face the issue. If he didn't understand it, so be it. She would have guilt and remorse but not forever. After all, he had been the one without the hard drive until lately.

Chip arrived while she was still on the balcony, poured himself a double shot of scotch and bottled bay water and walked tentatively to the balcony. He sat silently for awhile, but twisting back and forth in his chair. Finally he stood and arched his back. "Melody," he said, "You are the love of my life. I know I work too much and haven't showed much emotion until recently. But we're got to talk."

"You have been pretty attentive lately," Melody said. "But I know. We've got to talk and let's try to be reasonable, upscale people about this. After all, we have a touch of class."

Chip took in a deep breath and exhaled. "Yes," he said. "So let me say how deeply I am offended. Not at you, but at myself."

Melody took a sip of wine. "Do we have to talk about it?" she asked.

"Yes," he said. "Because your health is involved. I've got to he open with you." He threw his face into her lap and nuzzled, hoping for a maternal stroke that might help. "I am so sorry, Melody." He nibbled at her bathrobe that was cinched tight.

"I am too," she said. "But what can I say? Things happen."

"Let me be open and honest," Chip said. "You know all this crap that's going around about being nice to Tourists?"

Melody nodded.

Chip continued, "The other day there was this woman in the Grand Cove Bank. I think it was the day you lunched with your friends. I was in the lobby doing something. She seemed a little disoriented and I asked if I could help. She said she was down for a brief visit and was trying to cash an out-of-town check. She had forgotten her ATM card or something. She said she was from Dallas. Her clothes looked very Nieman Marcus. She had this sexy, Texan drawl. 'I want to cash this little check here with you. It's as good as I am,' " she told me.

"Well, we got her check cashed and I walked her to her car. She invited me for a drive to show her around Grand Cove. I was just wanting to be nice to a Tourist so I went with her," Chip continued, talking to her left thigh. "We ended up in a motel."

"Did you use a rubber?" Melody asked.

"No," he said. "I didn't. I guess I just got caught up in the emotion of getting some strange or doing my civic duty by being nice to a Tourist. I just don't know but I feel so guilty and realize how much I care for you. Everytime I thought of you I got really horny. That's why I'm been so active with you lately."

He continued, "But a couple of days ago when I was taking a leak I knew something was wrong and went to see Dr. Well."

"And?" Melody asked, readjusting Chip's head as it lay on her thighs.

"I've got gonorrhea," he said, continuing to talk to her thighs, afraid to look up and make eye contact. "Dr. Well gave me a shot and some medicine. He said you likely have it too. So you need to get treated. And let me tell you, Melody, if I ever see that Dallas bitch in Grand Cove again I'll use my computer system to get her credit rating and screw it up. That's how strongly I feel about it."

Melody stroked the back of his head as he burrowed deeper into her right thigh.

"I'm am understanding kind of woman," she said. "Not an approving one but an understanding one. Sometimes we all fall."

She lifted his head up. "Chip, why don't you make us a drink. We'll put this Be-Nice-To-Tourist Crap behind us and I'll get myself taken care of. OK?"

"OK," Chip said. "God, I love you. We'll get ourselves well and never look back. After all, we're on a journey. We need just to look ahead. We can't alter the paths we've taken but we can step more carefully in the future."

"And we will," she said. She wondered if she, too, should confess but decided against it. Too many confessionals might ruin a good relationship. And besides, she asked herself, who did what to whom? Was it him or was it her? Who caught what from whom?

"Chip," she said. "Get us that drink and let's sit and look at the bay and the moon."

Chapter 5   The Day That Santa Almost Died

Grand Covians awoke to the day after Thanksgiving with great anticipation. It was Parade Day. A banner in the Grand Cove Breeze heralded the event.

SANTA TO JUMPSTART GRAND COVE
He'll Chute into the City; Start Holiday Shopping Season

Sassy, Benny Slax, Botch and others on the parade coordinating committee gathered at 8 a.m. under a tent set up near the south end of Oyster Street, where the parade would begin, to go over final details. The group included the latest addition to the committee, Richard (Dick) Saldana Jr., president of the Grand Cove Jaycees, a swinging bunch who could bring new blood to the effort.

He was a big guy with a quick smile and even quicker handshake. He and his father, Richard (Dick) Sr., headed a law firm that specialized in personal injury claims, mostly from vehicle accidents. But they would file a claim about anything that would make a buck. To distinguish him from his father he was known around Grand Cove as Little Dick.

The committee huddled under the tent munching on breakfast tacos of potatoes and eggs.

A brisk northwesterly wind had blown in during the night and was whipping the palm fronds and flags toward the bay. Botch shivered a bit as he continued munching. They hadn't counted on a shift in wind patterns but it was not unusual and would keep everyone awake and alert. The morning was brisk but the sun was shining.

Botch and Sassy hunched over the run sheet that lay on a table. "All set, Sass?" he asked.

"Believe we're there," she said, dabbing at her mouth with a napkin. "Everything seems in place but flexible if we have to be." She pointed from the tent to an unmarked van near the kickoff point. "We've got that redundant Santa you wanted as a backup hidden in that van over there."

"Good," Botch said. "Can't be too careful. Always have a backup."

"We're gonna do good," volunteered Little Dick. "Hope there's no wrecks," he added and flashed a grin.

"Look at that crowd that's gathering," added Benny Slax. "I can almost hear the coins a jingling." He cupped a hand to his ear and smiled. Citizens were beginning to line the street. Those who had bought tickets were filling a viewing stand midway down the parade route. Store clerks stood at attention outside their businesses.

"Let's make it work and I wish everyone well," Sassy said. "I sure hope my new lines of stuff for the boys catch on." She smiled a bit mischievously. Sassy was using the occasion to expand her merchandise line to include something for teen boys and young men. She had added tee-shirts, jogging suits and other sweat wear to complement her swim suit lines, which featured the Grand Cove oyster designs. The apparel for the boys featured the phrase.

I'VE BEEN IN GRAND COVE:)

Sassy refocused on the run sheet and parade diagram. "Now let's look this thing over one more time," she said.

The parade would begin on the south end of Oyster Street, a block inland from Grand Cove Boulevard, and proceed north until it reached a dead end near the Port of Grand Cove.

The stage for the parade would be set by the parachute jump by Santa Claus, who would leap out of a light plane with a big gift bag on his back, and land on the esplanade, near City Hall. A team would escort him to the kickoff point for the parade.

A huge cardboard facade with a fireplace and candy canes painted on the outside had been placed across Oyster Street at the kickoff point.

At precisely 10 a.m. the Grand Covettes would kick through the facade and began prancing down the street, followed by the Grand Cove Municipal Band. Then would come Santa, who would walk merrily along and toss candies to the crowds lining the street.

After Santa would be Mayor Goodenough and members of CO-TIC, all in antique cars. Marching bands and cheer leaders from all of the high schools in the Grand Cove area would be spaced between the floats that would follow.

The parade was a democratic one, open to any group that could field a float. Sassy was pretty pleased with the lineup but not completely.

There would be a float bearing the Better Finks and one with the City Pretty Committee, sort of a one-person committee headed by Miss Lolita Gandy who had terrorized Grand Cove for many years about signs going up too close to the bayfront. She had been relatively inactive in recent years because there hadn't been much development and signs to promote them. She had raised hell about the mayor's balcony, to no avail in that case. But she knew how to attract attention.

Sassy had kept the parade order flexible with a major thought in mind. She had been searching for an Indian because bands of them, some friendly and some with cannibalistic tendencies, once roamed the area. It was so recorded.

"It would be a great to blend in some history with the start of the new millennium," she told her planning group on more than one occasion, but had no success at finding anyone who filled the bill.

Her cell phone rang as she and the group continued looking over final parade details.

"Great. Just great," she said into the phone. "Get him here as soon as possible and we'll have him cap off the parade."

The others were listening intently. "What's up?" Botch asked.

"Just great news," Sassy replied. "That was M.P. Booster on the phone. You know he's been working hard on getting us a new industry. I had told him jokingly that if he ran across a real, bona fide Indian in the process to let me know because we wanted one for the parade.

"Well," she continued. "He says he's got one and we need to get him in the parade."

"Tell us more," Benny Slax said, tugging at his left ear lobe.

Sassy continued. "M.P. said he got a call from a man who has been quietly visiting here. He is very interested in Grand Cove and on top of that he is a descendant of some Indian tribe that once lived in this area and wants to be in the parade."

"Will he be in full dress?" Botch asked. "You know, look like a real Indian."

"I assume he'll be in something," Sassy said. "But M.P. said it is very important that we let him in." She penciled in a last minute addition. "Parade closed by Indian Chief Harry Moccasin."

******

Sassy checked her watch. It was five minutes until Jump Time, when the plane carrying Santa would fly over the drop area and Santa would parachute onto the esplanade to start what they hoped would be the greatest shopping event in Grand Cove's not-so-glorious history.

She and the others looked toward the sky and in the distance they could see a plane approaching from the southeast, coming in over Grand Cove Bay toward the drop area.

"That's him," she shouted and jumped up and down, her substantial breasts jumping with her.

People lining the streets had also begun to look skyward.

The plane made a low pass over the area, wagged its wings and climbed back toward the sky.

"Ohhh," the crowd murmured. "Ohhh."

The plane made a large circular turn and headed back toward the drop area. A figured jumped from the plane and in no time the parachute filled out and the Santa figure began floating toward Grand Cove, bearing what appeared in the distance to be a large back pack.

"That's him," a kid shouted from a group assembled near a food booth. "That's Santa! I think I can see his beard and a toy bag." The others began waving and shouting, "Hello out there Santa." The northwesterly wind picked up their voices and carried them out over Grand Cove Bay, toward the Santa figure.

The Santa figure began to jerk as it descended toward the esplanada. The parachute seemed to be straining against the wind. It began to float farther out over the bay, pushed by the northwesterly wind. It moved farther and farther.

"What in the hell is going on?" Botch shouted. "The bastard is moving out instead of in."

"Wind's got him," Benny Slax said. "You think he'll be OK, what with that bag and all?"

"Where in the hell is Santa going?" Sassy said to no one in particular.

The plane made another circle and peeled off to the west, headed for the Municipal Airport where the flight originated.

Santa was being blown still farther out into the bay by the stiff wind.

"Oh my god," Sassy shouted. "He's not going to make it to the drop point."

Kids along the parade route began pointing. "Look," one shouted. "Santa's being blown away. Are we losing him?"

"No," another said. "He's always around this time of the year. What the hell kind of Christmas would we have without a Santa?"

Sassy got on her cell phone to the parade master. "Kick the goddamn parade off," she shouted. "And get that goddamn backup Santa into the lineup."

Within a few minutes the cardboard facade, almost exuding warmth with its painted fireplace and candy canes, was kicked open and the Grand Covettes pranced out, followed by the Grand Cove Municipal Band, which began playing "Here Comes Santa Claus."

The backup Santa followed the band, swaggering along in his Santa suit, tossing candies and trying mightily to shout "Ho, ho, ho" against the wind.

Mayor Goodenough followed in his antique car, waving a cowboy hat to the crowd and feeling a bit uncomfortable. He wasn't good at this sort of thing, he knew, but it was for the good of the city. He patted the flask of scotch and bay water that lay beside him to make sure it was there if he needed it.

The featured float of the parade, one designed by and built for the Grand Cove Junior League, was next. Amidst a group of the city's finest young women stood Melody, waving and laughing and pointing her forefinger and thumb pistol-like as she passed people she recognized. One thing she wasn't looking for was any goddamn Tourist strangers. But she did scan the crowds.

The Junior League float was followed by a tank made of cardboard and painted in primary colors. It was occupied by the Better Finks. Andrew Finke stood in the turret of the tank, waving an American flag. Others sat on the back saluting and also waving American flags.

They, like Miss Lolita and her City Pretty Committee, had been fairly inactive in recent years. His group had spent years searching high and low all over Grand Cove for a communist but without luck and things looked even dimmer with the collapse of the Evil Empire. But they continued to have their suspicions and never stopped looking. They bore their slogan with pride:

BETTER FINK THAN PINK.

Close behind was Miss Lolita and her float which was a decorated flatbed truck with a large sign poking into the air. "Signs Suck," it read. "And So Does Goodenough's Balcony." She held in her hands a smaller version which she jabbed into the air and wagged at the crowd as the float passed.

Feather sat in the reviewing stand along with some of Mayor Goodenough's aides, politely clapping now and then and wincing a lot as the parade contingents passed.

"What happened to the person who jumped out of the plane?" she asked one of them.

"Don't know," he replied. "Probably picked up by the Marina Patrol. "Great parade, huh?"

After most of the parade had passed their viewing area, they heard a loud whoop and saw a person in an Indian costume, including a full headdress of feathers. He was waving a tomahawk. He wore a placard that identified him as Chief Harry Moccasin.

He danced in a crouching motion and beat his palm against his mouth as he whooped and hollered and made his way down Oyster Street. "Harry here," he shouted now and again. "Harry in Grand Cove. Welcome Harry."

The crowds cheered him because they didn't know what else to do.

Feather, watching it all, said to no one in particular, "Excuse me, but what the hell is this?" No one answered.

The parade continued to wend its way down Oyster Street. As it ended, with Chief Harry Moccasin closing it out, the crowds began to make their way to the stores to get in on the early Christmas bargains. Clerks who had been standing at attention outside their stores began to open the doors to them. They had been busy earlier marking down prices that had been marked up to give the impression of one hell of a sale.

Chapter 6   **Report to the Mayor**

Mayor Goodenough sat on his balcony looking out over Grand Cove Bay, sipping on a scotch and bay water and awaiting the arrival of the Usual Suspects.

It had been three days since the Christmas parade and he wanted a report on how sales went and reports on other works in progress. He was, he had to admit, juggling a lot of balls at one time. He had headed out to his ranch right after the parade with orders he was not to be disturbed. He wanted to think there for awhile.

He briefly studied a seagull standing on one leg and wondered if it was the same one he looked at so often or if it was just passing through, on its way to somewhere far away.

He turned slightly as he heard the sliding door to the balcony open. Feather stepped out lightly and announced, as she always did, "They're here." Did he detect a touch of sarcasm?

"Send'em out," he said.

The group worked their way out onto the balcony and without waiting for an invitation from the mayor, for they knew by now none was needed, they helped themselves to scotch and bay water and took seats.

Botch took a tentative sip on his drink and winced slightly. He needed to stop pouring so strong. He nodded toward Sassy, "You want to lead off, Sass."

She nodded and walked to the outer railing, a notebook in her hand, and turned to face the group. The southeasterly breeze whipped lightly at her skirt. It was so short and tight the bay breeze did little to ruffle it but she reached down and gave it a tug.

"Thank you, Botch," she said and thumbed through her notebook. She looked up and smiled. "Mr. Mayor, I am happy to report our Christmas Parade was an unparalleled success."

Other members of the Usual Suspects nodded and rocked their bodies in their bolted chairs and took sips of their drinks.

"While I don't have any official numbers yet, the stores we surveyed all report a hellofva increase in early Christmas sales," she said. Despite her upbeat report there was something a bit subdued about her. Her eyes darted now and again toward Botch and Benny Slax. Her voice had lost just a little of its pitch.

"I sure did good," added Benny Slax, who had draped his left leg over the arm rest of his chair. "Great job, Sass," he added. And then, almost abruptly, he swung his leg off of the arm rest, as if he had been caught scratching his balls in public.

Botch sat quietly sipping on his scotch and bay water.

Sassy readjusted her stance, breathed and pulled her shoulders back, causing her breasts to strain at her blouse, as they always did. She took another deep breath. "I don't want to brag," she said. "This is a team effort for everyone. But I had a hellofva day. The guys were really snapping on my new outfits. You know, the ones that say, 'I've Been in Grand Cove.' "

"I think I've hit on an idea that people everywhere can get their hands around," she continued. "At some point I'm gonna take this puppy national," she said, nodding toward Botch as if to acknowledge she was picking up on one of his expressions. "Probably set up a web page and do some internet marketing. That Dell guy up around Austin sure made it work."

"Looks like we finally got one right," the mayor said.

Botch blushed slightly. "One of many we're gonna get right, your honor," he said. "One of many."

"But who was that weirdo of an Indian that closed out the parade. Never got to really see him because I took off right after my part ended?" the mayor asked.

Sassy nodded toward M.P. Booster and moved off to the side of the balcony railing.

M.P. arose from his chair, took a sip of his drink and cleared his throat.

"Not as weird as you might think," he said. "He may be the ticket to a new industry for Grand Cove. It could be really big." He paused for a moment to wait for reaction from the group.

"Wow, M.P. That's great. I knew you wanted him in the parade but didn't know we might be onto something big," Sassy said.

The mayor leaned forward in his chair. "Let's hear more," he said.

M.P. savored the moment and then strode in short, fat steps to the outer railing and turned to face the group.

"As you know I have taken the lead in trying to land us a new industry...something that will generate jobs...help get Grand Cove on the map," he began. "And as you know all of this industry recruiting business is hush-hush. Can't let the competition know what we're doing. And companies looking to relocate or do a startup don't want to tip their hands either.

"But I've been in touch with a group that wants to open a moccasin factory here in Grand Cove," he said. "Can't give any names cause I don't know them except for Harry Moccasin, who heads up the group. He was that quote weirdo unquote Indian. Claims to be a descendent of a tribe that once roamed this area. Says he has good backing from a group in New Jersey he wouldn't identify."

There were murmurs of approval around the chairs.

Feather arched an eyebrow.

"What would they make?" Benny Slax asked with a chuckle.

"They'd make Indian moccasins," Booster said with a straight face. "Real, honest-to-goodness moccasins. Authentic stuff. The kind real Indians wore. Its the kind of puppy we can really promote." He, too, nodded toward Botch, who gave a slight wave of his hand as acknowledgment.

Mike Wheelhorse, who rarely said much but listened intently, interrupted. He brushed his hand over his close-cropped hair. "What will they want in return?" he asked.

"Well," Booster continued, "the usual things that cities do these days. Probably some tax breaks...some land...nothing more than is asked of any city, and if this city is gonna grow - and it is - we oughta go after it."

"That should be something we can call promote," Wheelhorse said. "It doesn't duplicate any industry we already got. Wouldn't want to do that."

"Let's do what we have to do," Mayor Goodenough said. "Get some more details and we'll take it from there. Let's not lose a bird in the hand, or should I say a seagull in the hand." He chuckled at his attempt at humor and the others joined in.

"As soon as I get our gulls in a row I'm going to bring Harry in for a face-to-face meeting with all of you," Booster said. "He's anxious to meet."

"Anything else?" the mayor asked.

Botch half-rose from his seat. "We've been pretty wrapped up with the Christmas parade," he said. "And we'll have that eyesore along the State Highway from the airport taken care of soon. We've hired a contractor to put up a tall, redwood fence for a couple of miles to screen it off. We're still tinkering with some message we'll strip along the fence and after that we'll get her up. We'll drive you out soon so you can see firsthand."

"That's it for today, Mr. Mayor. Hope you had a nice rest out at the ranch," Botch added and got up as if to leave. He seemed more rushed than usual.

"Just one other thing," the mayor said. "What happened to that guy dressed like Santa Claus who jumped out of the plane. Last I saw he was being blown out over the bay. I assume the Marina Patrol got him out OK."

Botch glanced toward Sassy and Benny Slax.

"I almost forgot," Botch said. "So many things working." He paused and took a deep breath. "What happened to him is that we don't know what happened to him," he said.

"The boat from the Marina Patrol searched the area but came up empty. We contacted the Coast Guard to see if he may have drifted out over the Gulf. They didn't find anything either. We just don't know and our collective hearts are sad but hoping he is somewhere safe and sound. He was one of those transient Santas who look for work this time of year so we didn't have anyone to contact."

Botch paused again and looked out over the bay. "It was a good thing we had that backup Santa," he said. "The kids would of been really disappointed if he hadn't shown up."

Chapter 7   Chief Moccasin Meets the Mayor

M.P. Booster was excited and a bit apprehensive. He arrived early at City Hall and Feather had let him out on Mayor Goodenough's balcony. He poured a stiff drink of scotch and bay water and glanced out over the bay. His eyes fell on what appeared to be a one-legged seagull. He'd have to tell the mayor about that! But his thoughts quickly shifted back to the issue at hand - the meeting with Chief Moccasin. This would be the make or break meeting with the Chief to learn if the city would meet his requirements for a new factory. If the Usual Suspects signed off on it the formal approvals would be routine.

While there had been general concurrence, the nut-cutting details hadn't yet surfaced. Booster knew them, of course, because he had engineered the whole damn thing and his reputation as a prime mover and shaker was at stake. This was his baby and he didn't want it to abort.

Harry was asking for a lot, Booster conceded as he went over the pep talk he would make to the Usual Suspects. But on the other hand, Harry promised a lot. An even trade and a new industry for the city...the city that was gonna grow. It would help if he could get the goddamn Indian to speak in regular English, but you took things as they were and dealt with them. The Chief had flown in that afternoon and gone to his suite at the Sons Hotel, where Botch would pick him up for the meeting.

The balcony door slid open. Feather emerged and announced, "They're here." Mayor Goodenough ushered out Chief Moccasin and Botch, along with Wheelhorse, Benny Slax, Sassy, Pete Garcia and Little Dick, the new member of the Usual Suspects who helped a lot with the Christmas parade.

"Drink, Chief?" Botch asked as the group converged on the bar and began pouring themselves drinks of scotch and bay water and stirring them with their fingers, as they had seen the mayor do.

"Harry have drink," he said and stretched a big hand out to accept one that had already been poured for him. Up close he didn't look very Indian for he was on the pale side. His hair was blond. He stood about five-foot six and had large hands. He wore leather pants and a leather jacket with fringes and a pair of moccasins with tassels.

He took a pull on his drink and sighed. "Is good," he said. "Harry may like Grand Cove."

As the group took seats around the balcony, Booster took a position facing them, his back leaning against the outer railing. He tapped his glass for attention and cleared his throat.

"The mayor and I would like to thank all of you for gathering here for this historic occasion," he said. "As you know I have been leading the charge to get us a new industry, one of the three planks in our growth platform of Tourism, Industry and Conventions. Have been meeting with Chief Moccasin, quietly of course, and believe have plan that be good for Grand Cove." He paused for a moment and chided himself. Goddamn it, he was starting to talk like him. He took a sip of his drink to recover his faculties.

"Now, the city will have to do some things to make this work but we'll get a new industry and jobs out of the deal," he continued. "I've, of course, briefed Mayor Goodenough but we need the support of all of you. The chief will outline his proposal." He nodded toward Harry Moccasin. "Chief, tell us about it and a bit about yourself."

Moccasin arose and handed his empty drink glass to Botch who rushed to the bar to make another one while Moccasin strode to the end of the balcony. He looked out over the bay and turned slowly to face the group. "Harry like what he see," he said as he accepted his drink from Botch and took a sip.

"As some know, Harry want to build moccasin factory here but city must help. Harry need large piece of land near port for factory. City give land and build factory. Harry pay no taxes but create hundreds of jobs for people. Will call factory Harry's Moccasin Factory. Citizens must also show commitment by buying moccasins. Harry want moccasins on all feet. He believe city will support. Parade gave Harry chance to see community and he pick up good vibes. Believe city hungry for new industry."

Mike Wheelhorse cleared his throat for attention. "That deal seems fair. It's what other cities are doing. We build the factory and forgive the taxes and you create jobs. As an industrialist, one who has had his share of not being appreciated until recently, I like it. But how are you going to get our good Citizens to buy your product?"

"Harry have plan to make sales during dedication," the Chief replied. "City must help me promote. Also, Harry hire locals. Maybe work out payroll deduction so all can buy many pairs."

"As for self, Harry traces lineage back to the Coveanees. His ancestors were chiefs so Harry must carry on. Chief Harry also plan to create trust fund for education of descendants of the Coveanee tribe. That help sales."

Although she normally just sat as an observer, Feather raised her graceful body from her chair. "I thought the last vestiges of the tribe had long since disappeared," she said. "Have you new information?"

Chief Moccasin clutched his drink tightly and turned red in the face. He looked accusingly at Feather. "You census taker?" he asked.

"Just curious," she said. "And finally you're red."

"Now, now, Feather," Mayor Goodenough said gently. Botch retrieved the glass from the Chief's clutched hand and made him another drink. He seemed to regain his composure after taking a stiff pull on the fresh drink.

"Nother thing," he said. "Harry need sign to advertise factory. Assume that no problem."

"Well, all facilities have signs so that shouldn't be a problem," Benny Slax said. "I've got a modest one advertising my store and so does Sassy and all the others."

"What Harry have in mind modest by his standards. But Harry think big," Chief Moccasin said.

"Just so long as we don't get that Miss Lolita bitch riled up," Mayor Goodenough said.

Botch arose from this chair, "We can deal with it. We can deal with anything. We get this industry and we're well on our way to making this city grow."

"OK, then we'll deal with it," Goodenough said. "And our thanks to M.P. for his hard work in bringing this about. We'll let a contract and get this factory going up."

M.P. Booster beamed and waved a hand at the group as if to say he was just doing his job. He stood and held out his glass. "Join me, please, in a toast to Harry," he said. They all stood and raised their glasses of scotch and bay water. Booster turned to the Chief. "Welcome to Grand Cove, The City That is Gonna Grow," he said.

Botch couldn't help himself, seeing the first real leg of their tripod about to become a reality. All that crap about the allergy-prone, gay Tourist was behind them. The Tourism leg was already showing some signs of life and he had a grand idea for the Convention Center leg and he had taken care of that problem of slums and garbage dumps by the Grand Cove Airport.

"Join me," he shouted and hacked his hand down into the Grand Cove night air.

They recited the mantra.

> "The city, the city, the city
> A little bit down a pity
> For awhile we've been sucking hind titty
> But this town is gonna grow."

Botch turned and hurled his glass into the bay and the others followed, including Chief Moccasin who threw his left-handed and got the greatest distance.

Chapter 8   **Works in Progress**

Botch tooled his SUV down Grand Cove Boulevard and turned left to get on the State Highway. He and Mayor Goodenough were headed for the airport.

"You gotta see what we've done with that crappy view that our visitors see as they drive into the city," Botch said.

"It wasn't good," the mayor agreed.

"I think you'll like it," Botch said. "Also, I wanted to use this time to bounce another idea off of you in connection with our efforts to build a new convention center. Things are actually falling into place. Work'll be starting soon on Chief Moccasin's new factory. It won't take long. Throw up a big structure for his machines, recruit locals for the work and we're on our way."

"We need to keep cracking. The clock is running on us," the mayor said.

"Here's what I have in mind," Botch said. "There's an informal group of people associated with conventions who go around looking at potential cities to hold various major conventions. They're not official but they're all well connected with the people who make the decisions. I heard about them during my various promotion efforts. I'd like to bring them in for a visit to Grand Cove, get an informal recommendation from them that this would be a great site for a convention - great weather, a seacoast, a chance to combine official business with a vacation. Convention goers spend good because most are on someone else's expense account."

"And?"

"If we could get a mention, just a mention, we could use that as an incentive to build a new convention center. Of course, the convention site people will say the present center is not adequate but that we have big plans. The decisions on where such and such an association will hold its next convention is made several years in advance. So we bring in this group, get positive feedback and tell the voters we need to float a bond issue to build a new convention center with the almost certainty we'll be playing in the big leagues down the line."

"Just who is this group?" the mayor asked.

"As I said, it's real informal and doesn't have a name. They kind of float, but I can find them. A guy named Huey runs them."

"So what do we do?"

"They're pretty picky and used to good treatment so we'll have to send a plane to get them and set'em up in one of Pete's suites," Botch said.

"Sounds OK, " the mayor said. "We can send my private jet."

"I was hoping for that," Botch said. "Such perks go a long way."

Botch was rapidly approaching the Grand Cove Airport, which sat on their left heading out on the State Highway. On the right loomed a huge redwood fence, anchored at intervals by concrete posts. It stood about 12 feet high, effectively screening off the view of the slums and the garbage dump. Only a few scavenger gulls could be seen.

"This is it," Botch said, gesturing with his right hand. The fence was studded with continuing signs that illuminated at night when auto lights picked them up and were clearly visible during daylight hours.

"WELCOME TO GRAND COVE THE CITY THAT IS GONNA GROW. WELCOME TO GRAND COVE THE CITY THAT IS GONNA GROW. It went on for two miles, before the fence ended.

"So what do you think?" Botch asked.

"Not a very permanent solution," the mayor said. "But it solves an immediate problem."

"Now, Mayor, I have another idea we really need to focus on." Botch said.

"Let's hear it," the mayor replied.

"Well," Botch continued, "We've got this pretty crappy airport - not attracting the big airlines at all - but we can impress those who come in on the smaller collectors and parlay this into a big boost for downtown."

"I'm listening," the mayor said as Botch continued his drive toward the airport.

"This is what I have in mind," Botch said. "A Red Carpet to greet all of our visitors. We can lay down a thick piece of carpet that will extend from the airport terminal to the parking lot. Everyone will walk on Red Carpet whether they're coming or going. Our way of welcoming and saying goodbye."

"You mentioned downtown," the mayor said.

"This one's good," Botch said, gently patting the arm rest that separated them. "This one's good. We'll lay that same Red Carpet down Oyster Street with a little embroidered message on each end of every block. You can guess what it'll say. It'll say 'Welcome To Grand Cove. The City That is Gonna Grow.' "

"What will the carpet thing cost?" the mayor asked. "Some city council members are giving me a little flak here and there about a lot of public expense with nothing to show for it."

"It gets even better," Botch said. "We'll hold a fund raiser to pay for the carpet. Give everybody in Grand Cove a chance to be a part of the action. And I've got a plan for doing it. I'm getting some cost estimates and as soon as we get some of these other things rolling we'll start on the carpet."

The mayor sighed. "Well, why not. We're already in pretty deep. But we've got to start showing some results." His demeanor changed for a moment and he turned left and faced Botch, not smiling at all. "And I do want some results."

"We're covered," Botch said.

Chapter 9   **The Convention Committee**

"I've found the main group," Botch said to Mayor Goodenough as they rolled out once again toward Grand Cove Airport, where the mayor's private jet was hangared. "They've been hanging out in San Antonio - a great place to hang out, by the way, what with its River Walk and the Alamo. I've heard the San Antonio department that works on conventions have treated this group very well in terms of wining and dining and that is what they want."

"As I mentioned, I got hold of Huey on his cell phone," Botch continued. "They've agreed to come down and will be waiting for me at a private terminal at the San Antonio International Airport. I've talked with Booster about a reception committee when we touch down back here. And, of course, we need you as part of the welcoming group."

"Of course," the mayor said. "I'll be here." He paused for a moment and took a breath. "Botch, we really need to make this one work."

"Can't miss," Botch said with his usual enthusiasm. "We'll welcome them, take'em to the Rotary lunch, give'em a chance for a break at the Sons and them a tour of the city. And we'll do something special in the evening. Jenette and some of her girls from the port have already been contacted."

******

Botch strode with a hop in his gait, heading for the private terminal, after the mayor's jet touched down at the San Antonio International Airport. There was the buzz of traffic as cars entered and left the airport, some detoured by construction under way on the parking areas.

As he approached the terminal Botch could see a group sitting by a window with something in their hands. He quickened his pace. This has got to be the Home Run, he said to himself.

He entered the terminal and saw four men sitting on a couch and nearby chairs, sipping on something they poured from thermos bottles into paper cups.

Botch approached the group. "Huey, I presume," he said as he approached a man who was sitting in a chair away from the rest of the group. He seemed to be the leader.

"Yes," the man replied. "I'm Huey." Botch stuck out his right hand but dropped it after Huey made no attempt to shake it. Botch glanced at his watch. It was a little after ten in the morning.

"I'm Botch Botsford," Botch said. "You're gonna love Grand Cove. I got a plane waiting for you - Mayor Goodenough's private jet. First class or no class," he chuckled.

One of the men in the group poured refills. "Join us," he said.

"Or course," Botch said as one of them handed him a paper cup. He sipped it and recognized the morning snap of a strong Bloody Mary.

"Let me tell you a little about our plans," he said as the bite of the Bloody Mary rolled down his throat.

"They'll be a brief reception at the Grand Cove Airport and then a late luncheon at the Rotary Club. We'll give you a break in suites at our best hotel and then comes a tour of Grand Cove," Botch said.

Huey and his group sipped on their drinks and said nothing. "And tonight we've got a little private party planned at the hotel. You know the kind I'm talking about," Botch said and winked. Huey and members of the site committee smiled modestly.

Huey coughed softly against his hand. "Perhaps we could keep the tours and luncheons to a minimum," he said.

"But we want you to see what we got and what we have planned for the future," Botch said.

"We're sure everything is adequate or will be," Huey said.

Botch killed what remained of his drink and glanced at his watch. "Ready?"

"Very well," Huey said.

******

The welcoming committee at Grand Cove Airport waited anxiously. There were Mayor Goodenough, M.P. Booster, Sassy Butte and others, along with the Grand Covettes and the Grand Cove Municipal Band, which would perform as the site committee left the plane.

They heard a drone in the air and saw something in the distance. "Here they come," Sassy said, jumping up and down. "Here they come!" Her substantial breasts were bouncing.

Booster leaned over to the mayor and whispered. "Remember, I'll give the welcoming remarks. " The mayor nodded. "Whatever works," he said.

The plane touched down, bouncing a little on the runway as it landed. The band struck up a march tune and the Grand Covettes began twisting their butts and high kicking. A portable ladder was rolled to the plane to receive the guests. The welcoming committee followed.

Botch was the first to step out. He waved to the group as he descended the steps and stood at the bottom to help guide the others down.

"Welcome to Grand Cove," Booster said as Huey and his committee made their way onto the tarmac. "Welcome to the City That is Gonna Grow." He shot his right hand toward Huey's. But with a slow but deft movement Huey avoided it. However, Booster moved in quickly with his left hand and engaged Huey.

"Welcome, welcome," Booster said. "You're gonna like what you see and like what you hear about our plans for a new convention center."

Huey coughed on the back of his right hand.

"We're got limos waiting," Booster said. "The Rotary Club is waiting for us."

Huey frowned and pulled Botch aside. "The boys are a little tired," he said. "Could we pass on the Rotary thing?"

Botch flushed but quickly recovered. "You're the boss," Botch said and strode over to huddle with the welcoming committee.

"They're really beat," he said. "They been touring a lot of cities and just want to kick back. I've already got some inside info that they like us," he continued, breathing hard. "I'll get them situated in the Sons Hotel and you make our regrets to the Rotary," he said to Booster. "Let'em rest for awhile and then we'll do the tour." Booster frowned but nodded.

******

Booster stood before the Rotarians who had gathered in the banquet room of the Sons Hotel, where they meet monthly. After three men had stood and said they were visiting Rotarians who wanted to keep their never-missed-a-meeting record intact, Booster spoke to the group. "I have good news and bad news," he said. "The good news is that the Site Committee, which could bring us a major convention in the future and help us build a new convention center, is here. Right here in Grand Cove." There was applause while waitpersons stood in the wings to bring on the chicken and peas.

"The bad news is that the committee is so excited about visiting Grand Cove that they had to cancel this luncheon gathering." There were groans from the audience. "They're pretty tired from visiting so many cities they wanted a chance to catch their breath and read up on Grand Cove. And they'll be given a grand tour of the city after they rest a bit. I know they're gonna like it. I've already gotten some tips." He winked at the crowd and raised his arms as the waitpersons began to bring out the chicken and peas.

"Join me," he said and began the chant.

> "The city, the city, the city
> A little bit down a pity
> For awhile we've been sucking hind titty
> But this town is gonna grow."

The Rotarians responded with shouts and handclaps. Some held their arms into the air. "Now let's eat," Booster said.

******

Two limos pulled into the driveway of the Sons Hotel precisely at 2 p.m. Botch planned to put two Site Committee members in each limo. He and Sassy Butte would accompany two of them while Little Dick and Benny Slax joined the other two. They were the city's best promoters.

They assembled by the limos about ten minutes ahead of time to await the Site Committee. "They've had a couple of hours to rest so they should be ready," Botch said. He paced back and forth, glancing at his watch. Time passed and still no Site Committee.

At about 20 minutes after two he began to get agitated. "I better check on them," he said and headed for the 10th floor where the members had been put up in suites. He knocked on the door to Huey's suite. He got no response. He knocked again. "Huey, you in there?" He heard a noise from the other side of the door and then a voice. "Just leave the tray at the door and I'll get it later," said the voice, which Botch recognized as belonging to Huey. His words came out slow and thick. "I haven't got a tray," Botch said in a pitched voice. "It's me, Botch. Botch Botsford. It's time for our tour of the city."

"Just leave the tray by the door, Mr. Watchford. And tell the guy who's been serving us scotch and bay water to get some more up here. You're on to something with that bay water for a mix," the voice said.

"It's not Watchford. It's Botsford. You know, the guy who picked you up in the plane in San Antonio. We're going on a tour of Grand Cove, the city that is gonna grow. Don't you remember?"

"Frankly, I don't," Huey's voice said. "But if you say so I'll take your word. But we really need the scotch."

"Open the door, Huey. I really need to talk to you," Botch said.

"I'll open for scotch," the voice said.

"I'll be right back," Botch said, improvising as always. He ran down 10 flights of stairs, not remembering the elevator would have been faster.

He ran into the hotel bar and got two bottles of scotch from the bar manager. "It's an emergency," he said.

Clutching one in each hand he ran outside where Benny Slax, Sassy and Little Dick were waiting.

They gave him a puzzled look. "We got a minor problem," he said. "I'll be right back."

Botch bounded back up the stairs and was breathing hard by the time he reached Huey's suite. He rapped on the door.

"Just leave the tray by the door," Huey's voice said.

"It's not the waiter. It's me again. Botch. Botch with the scotch."

The door was cracked open. Botch got his foot inside and eased himself in. Huey wore a bathrobe and held a half-filled glass in his right hand. He motioned for Botch to set the bottles on a table. Huey twisted the top off of one of them and poured a stiff drink into his glass.

"Join me," he nodded toward Botch. "The boys have already passed out on me and I don't like to drink alone." Botch grabbed an empty glass from the table littered with food scraps and partially empty glasses.

Huey took a deep pull on his drink, sighed and wiped his mouth with the sleeve of the bathrobe. "Now what's this all about?" he asked.

"What's it all about!" Botch said, trying to contain his anger. His face was flushed. "What's it all about! It's all about Grand Cove and the tour we're supposed to take. You remember, you're checking us out as the site for a major convention somewhere down the line."

"Oh yes," Huey said. "We check out a lot of them. What was the name of this one again?

"Grand Cove," Botch said and took a deep pull on his drink. "Grand Goddamn Cove," he said. "We flew all the way to San Antonio to pick you up in the mayor's private jet."

Huey was quiet for a moment. He stroked his chin. "Oh, yes," he said. "It's coming back to me now. Dimly. But it's coming back. You were going to show us the city, entertain us and get us laid. Right?"

"And in that order," Botch said. "Speaking of getting laid, I feel like I just got screwed by you and your committee."

"Don't feel bad," Huey said. "It's happened to a lot of cities. Every damn one of them has a pitch. Me and the boys need something to do between conventions so we take what's thrown at us. It's a hellofva good deal." He stifled a burp.

"I can bet," Botch said. "So where does this leave us? You've got my ass way out on a limb."

"You look like a guy who can deal," Huey said and poured himself another drink. "Of course the tour of the city is out. We're not up to it. And we need to be at the airport in the morning. Nother group picking us up."

"Who? Botch said. "At least tell me who's our competition."

Huey pulled up the left sleeve of his bathrobe and glanced at a list of cities written on a band around his wrist.

He stuck his arm out to Botch. "I can't read this crap."

Botch stared in amazement as he looked it over.

"Why in the hell would you go to a town nobody can spell let alone pronounce?" Botch asked.

"Don't know?" Huey said. "I just call the plays. I'm just the quarterback. The boys over there do the detailed work." He nodded toward his passed-out committee members. "Where we headed next?"

Botch squinted at the arm band. "Looks like Waxahacia," he said. "Next thing you know you'll be getting a bid from Nocogdoches. Nobody can spell it either."

"It may be on the list," Huey said. "Like I said, I just call the plays and there's lots of folks out there with planes who want us to look them over."

"I feel like I've been given a royal screwing," Botch said. "I need to salvage something out of this."

"Like I said earlier," Huey said. "You look like a guy who can deal. Get us laid and to the airport on time and I'll see about putting in a word for - what is it again - Grand Grove?"

"Grand Cove," Botch said. "But I damn sure want that good word."

"You got it," Huey said and burped again. "But don't bet the farm on anything big happening here."

Botch fished his cell phone from his shirt pocket and called Jenette and told her to round us some of the Port of Grand Cove girls right away.

******

Botch returned to the driveway outside the Sons Hotel. The limos were still standing by, running up time. Benny Slax, Sassy and Little Dick had retired to the Moccasin Club.

Botch found them there, sipping on scotch and bay water, served in glasses holstered in leather covers with an imprint of a moccasin on them.

"So what the hell is going on?" Sassy asked, taking a deep breath after a pull on her drink.

"'Yeah?" Benny Slax repeated. "What in the fuck is going on." He blushed slightly for it was not like him to use profanity. But circumstances warranted it.

"It's kind of a screwed up story," Botch said. "But we'll salvage something. They're gonna pass on the tour and head out in the morning. I'll get Peewee - Sergeant Ratlidge - and some of his boys to take them to the airport. I can assure you that they're going to put in a good word for Grand Cove," Botch continued.

"But the mayor is gonna be pissed," he added.

Chapter 10   **Report to the Mayor**

The mayor was pissed.

He sat on the balcony outside his office at City Hall, clutching a drink and studying his one-legged seagull, an exercise that sometimes helped him control his inner rages.

He was, without question, pissed. There were already rumors among those in the know in Grand Cove that the Site Committee visit was nothing short of a major fuckup. He had his sources. Pete Garcia had filled him in a little, telling him about the huge amounts of scotch ordered from the Moccasin Room at the Sons Hotel. And, he relayed, Jenette and her girls emerged from the hotel the next morning looking all worked out.

The mayor recalled the phone conversation. "You know what she told me?" Pete had said to the mayor. "She said that was the horniest group they had ever met. Even halfway passed out and drunk they performed all night. The girls went there on good faith. They haven't seen a dime so far and they want to be taken care of. And what the hell have we got out of this?"

The mayor finished off his drink and walked to the bar to make another one.

******

The sliding door to the balcony opened and Feather stepped out. "They're here," she said. "They're here again."

"Send 'em out," the mayor said. He glanced out over the bayfront and saw the seagull he was studying take flight, with both legs visible. He managed a chuckle.

Botch, Sassy, Booster, Benny Slax and Little Dick Saldana walked out onto the balcony and all headed for the wet bar to make themselves drinks.

The mayor leaned on his forearms on the balcony rails, looking out over the bayfront, watching the whitecaps lapping against the seawall, the flutter of seagulls and the sun passing over City Hall, heading to the west. Well, he said to himself, at least we got this no matter what happens.

Botch downed a double and was making a refill. He cleared his throat as the others took seats facing the bayfront.

"I have some good news," he said.

Mayor Goodenough turned from the balcony and faced them. "Of course, you do. That is your job. You're supposed to bring good news. So let's hear it."

Botch blanched. Sassy, casting him a sidelong glance of sympathy, bounded up from her chair. "It's not that bad, your honor. We just got trapped up with some hustlers. But Botch says it's gonna work out."

Botch was on his third drink by now. "Mr. Mayor," he said, "You know that this promotion business has its ups and downs. I'm not going to try to tell you that it went just as we planned. But we salvaged something. That's the good news."

The mayor arched an eyebrow.

"The Site Committee has promised to put a good word for us as the place for a future major convention, and also that we're a good place to visit just like we are, " Botch said.

"How do we know that?" the mayor asked.

"Peewee - Sergeant Ratlidge - told me," Botch said. "I had him and his boys drive them to the airport and to drop a couple of suggestions along the way."

"And everything else is falling into place," Botch continued. "The Moccasin Factory is under way. Won't be long until we're got the machines humming and people here at work. We're working on a great dedication ceremony. Yessir, we gonna be in business once that factory is complete. And the monument to Harry Moccasin is beginning to take shape. He likes it."

"Any problems?' the mayor asked. "The last thing I want is any problems."

Botch swallowed.

"None really except for these people who constantly try to undermine the city - the city that is gonna grow," Botch said.

"Like who?" the mayor asked.

"Well, I've heard that Miss Lolita is snooping around the plant site and making snide remarks about the Harry monument. But that's minor. We can deal with her. And we're moving ahead with the Red Carpet. I've got some estimates and am working with Pete Garcia and the others here to launch a major fund raiser," Botch said.

"Little Dick says he can get his Jaycees behind it and Pete is gonna help us with a display area in front of the Sons hotel. And we're gonna hire a fund raising expert. Of course he'll take a little off the top but he'll get the job done," Botch continued.

"Won't be long before anyone who sets foot on Grand Cove Airport is going to step on a red carpet and when anyone is downtown they're going to walk the distance of Oyster Street on a red carpet, too. Mr. Mayor, we're gonna turn this village into the country's best known secret."

The mayor downed his scotch and bay water and stared at the group. "No more screwups," he said.

"Believe in it," Botch said. "In fact tomorrow I'd like to take you on a tour of Harry's factory. I know you're busy but this will give you a good update, one you can pass onto any complainers."

"Be nice to see some progress," the mayor said.

"I'll pick you up in the morning," Botch said. "You'll see the progress we're making."

The mayor nodded and turned to Feather. "You plan on coming along," he said.

"Of course," she said. "I want to see this progress, too."

Chapter 11   Miss Lolita

Botch arrived at City Hall early the next morning and bounced into the building. When the mayor sees the factory going up he'll forget all about that Site Committee thing, he said to himself. He'll see real progress.

He had the first-floor secretary call the mayor's office and advise that Botch was waiting downstairs to take him on the tour. Shortly, Mayor Goodenough and Feather emerged from the elevator.

"All set, Mr. Mayor?" Botch said. The mayor nodded and strode briskly toward Botch's SUV, Feather at his side, matching him stride for stride.

Botch drove north on Grand Cove Boulevard, towards the Port of Grand Cove, where the factory was being erected. In the distance, they could see something that seemed to be poking itself into the Grand Cove skyline.

As they neared they could see signs of construction - trucks coming and going and workers moving about and they could clearly see the thing that was poking itself into the skyline.

"What in the hell is that?" Feather asked.

"Oh, that," Botch replied. "That's the statue of Harry Moccasin. He refers to it as a monument. It went up first, at Harry's request."

As they arrived at the factory site they could see the likeness of Harry in all its glory. It stood about 50 feet tall, shaped in the form of a totem pole. At the top was a big head with a prominent nose that looked out over the bay. It looked like Harry Moccasin.

"Things are really moving along," Botch said. "These things can be put up pretty quick. A concrete floor, sides and a roof. Then we'll bring in the machines and the other stuff. And then," he paused for moment and took his hands off the steering wheel, "and then we're gonna be in business. We're gonna have the best moccasin factory in the country. There'll be jobs, people working and spending money. Yessir, Mr. Mayor, when word gets out, this town is gonna really grow." He was waving his hands.

"Careful," said the mayor, who was riding shotgun in the front seat. He grabbed the steering wheel to steady it as the SUV lurched to a halt at the entrance to the work site. They heard a noise coming from the outside of the SUV.

Botch could see the tall, thin frame of Miss Lolita who was beating on the vehicle with a sign. "So you're killers, too," she shouted and continued beating the vehicle with her sign. "You almost ran me down."

Botch shot the mayor a quizzical look and rolled down the window. "Just take it easy, Miss Lolita. We didn't mean to scare you."

"It's that goddamn sign that scares me," she shouted and slammed the SUV once more with her sign.

"Step back, we're coming out," Botch said. He let himself out on the driver's side while the mayor eased himself out on the passenger side and held out his hand to Feather to help her down.

"What's this all about, Miss Lolita?" the mayor asked as the group gathered a few yards from the SUV. Miss Lolita was disheveled and breathing hard.

"What's it all about? What's it all about? It's about the crappy sign sticking up in our skyline. That's what it's all about. And I'm going to picket this place until it comes down." She thrust her chin out and up. "And I can import other people. The City Pretty Committee considers this a major cause." She cut her head to one side and said almost in a whisper. "I've been in touch with some anarchists from Seattle."

Feather picked up the remnants of Miss Lolita's sign that were broken by the bashing on the SUV but she could still read the message: "That Stupid Sign of Harry Moccasin Sucks. Harry Moccasin Sucks." She winced and showed it to Botch and the mayor.

"Yeah," Miss Lolita shouted at them. "The whole damn thing sucks."

"Work with us, Miss Lolita," Botch said. "It's not that bad and Harry won't like you picketing here. Besides, the sign looks just like Harry."

"That's one reason it is so damn ugly," she said. "That fake Indian has already been out here to threaten me. He came out late yesterday right after I got here. He threatened me. And he threatened Grand Cove. Said he'd pull out of Grand Cove in a New York minute if I didn't get out of here." She glared at the three of them. "And I ain't going. That goddamn sign is what is going. He also said something about me swimming with the fishes."

Mayor Goodenough maintained his silence and he thought he heard Feather giggle. At least she had put her hand over her mouth.

"We'll take care of it," Botch said. "Now, Miss Lolita, why don't you just give yourself a break and we'll be in touch."

She took a deep breath and retrieved what was left of her sign. "I'll give you 48 hours or this 'Native American' project is history. I'll drive that fake Indian off."

Botch reached out to her and placed his right hand on her shoulder. "We'll work it out," he said. "You're a good person and this project is good for the city, the city that is gonna grow."

"You're on notice," she said and shook a bony fist at them. "I've already told that faker he sucks."

******

"So everything's on track," the mayor said sarcastically as Botch headed back to City Hall. "Everything is on track."

Botch stared straight ahead.

"The monument or whatever you call it is a bit much," Feather volunteered.

"The factory is good for the city," Botch said. "And Harry demands it." His mind was spinning. Mayor Goodenough sat silent. "We need to get this little problem out of way and we can do it," Botch said.

"How?" the mayor said. "No pun intended." He allowed himself a chuckle.

"We're gonna have a major meeting this afternoon in the Sons Deal Room. We need a quiet back room away from Harry and everyone else to work this out. I'll take care of the invites. I got a good plan," Botch said.

"It better be good," the mayor said.

******

Pete Garcia ushered the group into a remote back room, one reserved for deals and dealing. That's why it was known as the Deal Room. Mayor Goodenough, Botch, Sassy, Benny Slax, Booster, Mike Wheelhorse and Little Dick Saldana seated themselves in a large leather booth. A waiter bought drinks of scotch and bay water, served in leather covers with the imprint of a moccasin on them. That had become the standard at the Sons Hotel and was spreading to bars whose owners wanted to be a part of the movement to help the city grow. Pete had also taken to wearing moccasins he bought somewhere.

Botch raised his glass to them and took a pull on his drink and swallowed. "We're gathered here because we got a slight problem. The mayor and I checked it out this morning and we need to get it resolved right away or risk losing our moccasin factory."

"So what's the problem?" Sassy asked, leaning slightly over the tabletop, revealing the swell of her breasts. All eyes cut to them.

"The problem," Botch said, "is Miss Lolita. She is picketing the moccasin factory and says she will raise holy hell if the Harry Moccasin monument doesn't come down. And that sign is important to Harry. So I been thinking of how to placate her, how to help get her a life."

The others listened.

"I been thinking and what I been thinking is this: Why is Miss Lolita out there carrying a picket? Why isn't she at home worrying about the kids and school violence, going to PTA meetings and the like. Why? Because she is Miss Lolita. Miss. I think she needs a man. And we got to supply him," Botch said.

Benny Slax, Booster, Mike Wheelhorse and Little Dick shot each other glances. Sassy leaned over the table again. "Why's she got a problem? I'm a Miss and it's certainly not a problem for me." She let out a hearty laugh. The others chuckled but without conviction.

Botch cut his eyes toward her bosom. "Well, you're something special, Sassy. Also you're smart and got a going business." Sassy allowed herself a modest smile.

Little Dick broke out in a laugh and slapped his hand on the table. "A man for Miss Lolita. Who'd want to get tied up with that thing? I wouldn't screw her with your dick, Botch." He laughed and slapped the table again.

Botch continued, "Not only a man but someone she will respect, someone who is part of this noble effort to grow the city." There was a heavy silence.

"With someone to wine and dine her, to take her around the town, and who knows what else, she won't have time to worry about signs," Botch continued. "It may take a little sacrifice on the part of someone but it is for the good of the city, the city that is gonna grow."

Sassy giggled, "You volunteering, Botch?"

He turned white. "Don't kid about that. Don't even kid. I got my hands full just trying to keep everything coordinated. But it needs to be done." Everyone fell silent again.

The silence was broken as Pete Garcia came rushing into the room. Everyone looked up. "He's here, he's here," Garcia panted. "I tried to keep you hidden but Harry found out."

A loud whoop resounded to every corner of the Deal Room and Harry Moccasin strode in, wearing his Indian headdress. He stalked up to the table. "Harry been looking for you. Harry been all over town. Harry been making phone calls. Nobody know where nobody is," he shouted. "Maybe nobody like Harry."

"Just a little planning session, Harry," Botch said. "Of course everyone like Harry. Harry bringing in new factory."

"Then why city letting skinny bitch make fun of Harry and picket his factory and say ugly things about Harry monument?" Harry Moccasin asked. "Harry really wonder if city like him."

Benny Slax pushed back his chair and said in his smooth voice, "Everybody crazy about Harry. We just learn about Miss Lolita problem. Meeting now to deal with it." The others nodded and took strong pulls on their drinks. A waiter appeared and handed one to Harry. "Monument stay or Harry go," he said and downed his drink in one big swig.

"Of course monument stay," Botch said. "City have plan to take care of Miss Lolita."

"You let her swim with fishes?" Harry asked. "That take care of problem." He was beginning to settle down a little but remained standing. He held out his empty glass and a waitperson immediately took it and replaced it with a full one.

"City working on problem," Sassy said. "But we not barbarians. No swimming with fishes. We have much nicer solution. More fun, too." Harry approached an empty chair and kicked it, sloshing his drink in the process. He kicked it again. "So Harry now a barbarian. He getting more and more convinced city no like him."

Sassy leaned over the table, way over the table, so that Harry had a good view of her. "It just figure of speech, Chief Moccasin," she said. "City mean no harm."

"Then get problem solved," he said, cutting his eyes toward Sassy's interior. "Deal with it. And get rid of Lolita sign that say Harry sucks." He seemed to redden a little.

Botch got out of his chair, walked to Harry and put his arm around him. "City deal with it. Blood brother promise," he said.

"Harry don't want to see skinny bitch near plant again," Harry said. He finished off his drink, kicked another chair, whooped and strode out.

Botch remained standing. Right after Harry slammed the door behind him, Botch addressed the group. "As you can see, we have a problem. Miss Lolita's promised to stay away from the plant site for just 48 hours so we have to move quickly. We got to get her a man right away."

"What are your thoughts, Mr. Mayor?" Botch asked.

Mayor Goodenough took a pull on his SBW. He wiped his mouth with his sleeve. "My thoughts are these. I want this goddamn problem taken care of. I don't want anymore fuckups. Those are my thoughts." He was breathing heavily. "Those are indeed my thoughts."

Botch blushed slightly and wiped his hand over this head. "As I said we got to have a very special kind of person and that person is right here in this room."

The silence was deafening as Botch looked around the table. The men were clinching and opening their fists, none making eye contract with another.

Botch cleared his throat. "I've taken a lot of things into account, like who can sweep Miss Lolita off her feet."

He continued to look around the table. "I know all of you will join me in nominating Little Dick Saldana for the job." The others let out audible sighs.

"Excellent choice," Booster said. "Little Dick, his dad and family have always been there for Grand Cove."

"I agree one thousand percent," Benny Slax said.

"And I can tell you that as an industrialist I am solidly behind this nomination," added Mike Wheelhorse. "I know what it is to make touch decisions."

"He's certainly the best looking of the bunch," commented Sassy. The others cleared their throats.

"I'll get Miss Lolita set up," Botch said. "I'll handle all the details."

Little Dick just sat there. His fists were clinched and his knuckles white. His eyes jutted to one side and he looked strange indeed. He attempted to say something but no words came out.

Mayor Goodenough walked over to his chair and draped a long arm around him. "I know we can count on you, son. Grand Cove needs you."

Little Dick managed a nod. As the meeting ended each man walked by Little Dick's chair and pressed his shoulder. Sassy bussed him on the check. He was still sitting there, motionless, as the others left the room.

Chapter 12   The Red Carpet

Botch was in fine spirits as he entered City Hall for a briefing session with the mayor and the Usual Suspects. Things were looking up. He had good things to report. He joined most of the others in the waiting room of the mayor's office.

The mayor had retired to his balcony just after five to await them.

He watched his favorite seagull and wondered what Grand Cove and the rest of the country were coming to. Every time he was on a street he encountered oversized pickups or attack SUVs, the latter often driven by women with cell phones stuck in their ears, the former by overweight men wearing baseball caps. Maybe the country ought to declare a war and requisition all of the vehicles for use as tanks, he thought. The least he could do, he continued with one of his periodic thoughts of the day, is ban them from places like Oyster Street. He quickly dismissed the notion. Too many shoppers came to shop in their huge vehicles. He heard the glass door slide open.

"They're here," Feather said.

"Send'em out," he said and walked to the wet bar to mix himself a SBW.

The Usual Suspects filed out and headed for the bar to make themselves a drink.

After all of them had relaxed into a bolted-down chair and took appreciative sips of their SBWs, the mayor tapped his glass with his left thumb nail.

"Let's hear it," he said.

Botch arose from this chair and walked to the balcony's edge, measuring his steps. He turned and faced the group and held up his glass.

"No bad news," he said to the group. "Just good news." He glanced toward Mayor Goodenough and smiled.

"I am happy to report to all of you that Miss Lolita has withdrawn herself and her stupid signs from the factory site," he said. "Harry happy." There were mummers of approval.

"Cool, Botch, cool," Sassy Butte said. "That's just too cool."

She glanced around the balcony for a moment. "By the way, where is Little Dick?" she asked.

"He's busy," Botch said and winked. "He's real busy." There were snickers all around the balcony.

"OK," the mayor said. "Good that you got that issue worked out. Now let's hear the rest."

Botch took a light sip on his SBW, which he held in his left hand. He held out his right one and made a sweeping motion. "Mr. Mayor, we're on track with plans for the Red Carpet - the Red Road to Progress we're gonna call it. I've already added a little something extra for special visitors," he continued.

"Tell me more," the mayor said.

"As all of you know we do get some conventions, small ones, mind you, and an occasional businessman flying in. We're keeping tabs on all of them so I've hired a photo company to take pictures of them when they get off the plane. The picture takers wear badges around their necks so they look like newspeople. They snap pictures of the dignitaries. These people think the Breeze or somebody is taking note of their arrival. Impresses the hell out of them," he said.

"What happens?" Benny Slax asked.

"Nothing happens," Botch replied. "But it impresses."

"But on with the major news. We have a series of bids for installing the Red Carpet - at the airport and on Oyster Street. And I've hired a real fund raiser to finance the project," he said. "This will be something of and by the people."

"Who did you get?" asked Mike Wheelhorse as he passed his hand over his close-cropped hair. "I'm sure the employees of our industrial district will support any reasonable effort."

"He's an experienced fund raiser," Botch said. "Course he's got to get paid so he'll rake some off the top. But I've checked him out and this guy delivers. Don't know much else about him.

He lives in the Nevada desert and has a pager. He called and agreed to take on the project. I've sent him some background info."

"He have a name?" Benny Slax asked.

"He's known as the Mack the Money Man," Botch said. "He's got some good ideas. First, we're gonna set up one of those signs that look like a thermometer. As the money flows in the thermometer will rise so folks will know how the campaign is progressing. We're also gonna put in a barrel next to it so people can drop in cash."

He looked toward Pete Garcia who had taken a brief break from his hotel to attend the meeting. "Pete's agreed to let us put the thermometer sign and barrel in front of the Sons Hotel. There's a lot of drop by traffic there," Botch said.

Pete Garcia nodded. "What's good for the city is good for the Sons," he said. "By the way," he said, cutting his eyes toward Botch. "Jenette is really bugging me. The girls haven't been paid for that visit of the Site Committee and I'm not going to take the hit for it."

"Front'em Pete and we'll build it into the Red Carpet fund raiser," Botch said. "You'll get your money back. I'd paid it out of committee funds but what if the word got out we were paying for this sort thing."

"That's fine," Pete said. "I'll just lift my cut right out of the donation barrel. Not a skim but a payback." There were nods around the group.

Mayor Goodenough finished his SBW and walked to the bar. "I haven't really heard a plan," he said. "I've heard a lot of bullshit. How is this Money Man guy gonna raise the money beside that barrel thing?"

Botch strode from one end of the balcony to the other.

"Mr. Mayor," he said with conviction, "the plan we're working on will work. And everyone in Grand Cove gets to be a part of it. Money Man's plan is to sell a square foot of the Red Carpet to each and everbody in Grand Cove. The slogan will be, 'Buy Your Fair Square.' "

"He ever work for the United Way?" Sassy asked and smiled.

"He's worked for many successful fund raising groups," Botch said. "The Breeze has agreed to run a series of articles promoting the event," he continued. "We'll kick it off next Monday with a press conference and we'll need all of you there. Money Man is driving in this weekend to get things totally under control. That's it from my end. I'll now call on M.P. to fill you in on what the Chamber of Commerce is doing to help in this effort."

M.P. Booster nodded and eased himself out of his chair. He sighed from the effort and walked out to where Botch was standing. Botch stepped a foot sideways and took a pull on his SBW.

Booster cleared his throat. "I'm happy to report that the Grand Cove Chamber, as always, is solidly behind this effort, as it is for anything that is good for the city and good for business. We've been in touch informally with our membership and their companies have agreed to send letters to all of their employees urging them to participate through payroll deduction. A good, clean way that has worked in many other endeavors," he said.

The others nodded. "Good work, M.P.," Benny Slax said. Booster acknowledged them with a wave of his fat left hand and walked back to his chair.

Botch stepped up to face the group. "We need to keep tight control over this. Let's meet next Wednesday for lunch at the Sons. I'll bring along the Money Man so all of you can meet him.

******

Pete Garcia ushered the Usual Suspects back into the Deal Room as they arrived for lunch. Botch, feeling really good, came early and was standing at the doorway to the club to greet them.

The Money Man stood beside him. He was a tall person with an angular chin. His hair was pulled back into a pony tail. His light blue eyes were always in motion, darting here and darting there. He wore a suit without a tie and casual slippers without socks.

Botch had brought along copies of the Tuesday edition of the Grand Cove Breeze in case anyone needed an extra one. He glanced again at the headline of the banner story they scored from the press conference on Monday.

CITY UNVEILS PLAN TO PROMOTE CITY
Will Follow Red Road to Progress

Waitpersons brought in SBWs as the group seated themselves in a circular booth at the back end of the Deal Room, the quiet place where they could talk business, away from the trouble makers.

Botch stood after the others were seated. He nodded down to the stack of newspapers. "I assume you all saw the story in the Breeze. Mr. True had promised us support and here it is. He's True to his word, so to speak."

He looked down at his left. "Let me introduce the man who will head our fund raising effort - Mack the Money Man from Nevada," Botch said. The Money Man nodded as he lifted his lank body from his chair.

"Thank you," he said, his eyes darting around the table. "I believe we have a very doable project here. You're fortunate you have a person like Mr. Botsford here in Grand Cove. After meeting with him I know he knows his business." Botch allowed himself a beam.

"I've been in the fund raising business for awhile," Money Man continued. "It is, in fact, my calling. I love to raise money. And I can tell you there is competition for dollars from the working people but I think we can build on this 'Buy Your Fair Square' approach."

"As you know the United Way has had success with similar slogans. What we want to do is roadblock the citizens. Everywhere they turn they'll be asked to give - to take part, if you will - in this Red Road to Progress. We'll have TV spots, ads in the Breeze and volunteers from various organizations waving squares of carpet to catch people as they come into Pete's great hotel here," he continued. "We might as well let the visitors help pay for this thing. Also, the Fire Department has agreed to have its people stand at intersections on weekends holding their firefighter boots to accept donations from motorists."

Sassy waved her hand. "And don't forget us," she said.

Money Man cut his eyes toward her. "Of course not," he said. "Ms. Butte and Benny Slax have also agreed to have auxiliary barrels set outside their stores to pick up anyone we may have missed. They generate a lot of traffic."

Sassy and Benny Slax smiled. "We try," Benny Slax said. "We try hard."

Money Man's presentation was interrupted by a knocking at the door to the Deal Room. It was a heavy knock. There was a faint voice audible from outside the heavy door. "Open up you bastards, you left-leaning sons-of-bitches, you goddamn traitors," the voice said.

"What in the hell is that?" Mayor Goodenough asked. "Just what in the hell is that?" The noise continued. Finally the door opened and Pete Garcia fell to the floor from a cane blow to his left leg, a cane wielded by Andrew Finke. "They found us," Pete said, holding his leg in pain.

Andrew Finke, accompanied by four old men wearing "Better Fink Than Pink" caps, limped into the room. Andrew Finke was swinging his cane above his head. "Why you," he said to no one in particular. Money Man grabbed an ash tray and began backing off. Botch stood up and was swatted on the right shoulder by a cane. "Why you," Andrew Finke said again.

Sassy Butte stood up and thrust out her breasts. "What in the hell is going on here, Andrew." The old man couldn't help but glance, however, duty pressed him on.

"What in the hell is going on? How dare you ask, Miss Big Butte? You know what in the hell is going in. This city is being turned back to the communists. A Red Road to Progress. A Red

Square for everyone. I knew it in my bones. I knew something was fishy in Grand Cove."

The mayor felt the pressure of leadership. He nudged Feather who stood and looked at Andrew Finke. "Mr. Finke, what in the hell is the problem?"

"Miss Feather I got no argument with you. You've got all that book learning and stuff and seem like a sensible young lady but this damn Red Carpet is too much. You know as well as I do that the Red Threat is still out here. And we are going to take it laying down. I mean really laying down. Whereever your left-leaning cronies try to lay a piece of Red Carpet we're going to be in front of the equipment, laying down so your bulldozers can crush us. We are men of sacrifice."

And he added, "We're going to contact important foundations - those that study leftists. And we're going to be in touch with important publications that have not steered from their views."

Feather remained standing. "Mr. Finke, regardless of what you think about the Cold War, it is over. These people here are just trying to do what they think is best for Grand Cove." He studied her for a moment. "So you've been brain-washed too," he sneered. Botch made an attempt to stand up. "Why you," Andrew Finke said, waving his cane. Botch retreated to his chair while Money Man stood on the side, in a defensive posture and still clutching an ash tray. Andrew Finke continued glaring at them while his Better Fink colleagues stood rigidly by the door.

"Mr. Finke," Feather continued. "We can work out something. I usually don't get involved but we really like and respect you. Why don't you and your buddies join us at this table and have an SBW."

"What's that?" he asked.

"The national drink of Grand Cove," she said. "I'm sure we can work something out. You know the city loves you."

Andrew Finke took a deep breath. "I don't know what we can work out but I'll listen. I've been after the Reds for a long time and I believe we have scored."

Feather took her seat beside the mayor.

Goodenough whispered in her ear, "Thanks. I know it was a chore," he said. She nodded.

Andrew Finke waved the other Better Finks over and settled down a bit as all of them sipped on SBWs. "Look," he said. "I don't want to have myself crushed by heavy equipment but we conservatives got to have something to hold onto. I love Grand Cove but I don't want it going Red - or Pink, for that matter. We need something to hang onto."

Money Man was still standing in the corner, clutching an ash tray, his eyes darting here and there. He motioned Botch to come over and whispered in his ear, his eyes still darting. They talked in hushed tones. Botch motioned Feather to join them. The three of them continued talking in low voices.

When they finished Feather motioned to Andrew Finke. "Join us, please, Andrew," she said. He stalked over. She led him away from the group and talked with him privately. Andrew Finke listened intently and then nodded. Feather guided him back to the table where the rest of the Usual Suspects were waiting and watching. She nodded to Botch. Botch and Money Man made their way back to the table.

Botch remained standing. He looked around the table and cleared his throat. "I'm glad to welcome the newest member to our group," he said. "Mr. Finke, I'm glad to say, is going to help us in our fund raising effort. He's on our side." Andrew Finke managed a nod.

The others at the booth applauded.

Sassy, as usual, broke the silence. "What's he gonna do?"

"You'll see," Botch said. "We're on our way."

Andrew Finke walked to each of his colleagues and whispered in their ears. They nodded and signaled for another round.

******

A big red ribbon was stretched across the south end of Oyster Street. And as far as the eye could see there was a carpet, reaching all the way to the end of Oyster Street near the Port of Grand Cove. Crowds lined the sidewalks. The street had been cordoned off. The carpet was durable outdoor carpet that had been compacted upon an asphalt base. It was thick enough to feel a little soft to the foot and durable enough to handle vehicles, at least for awhile.

The Grand Cove Municipal Band and the Grand Covettes stood behind Mayor Goodenough and other dignitaries as they prepared to snip the ribbon to officially inaugurate the opening of the Grand Cove Carpet to Progress, as it had been renamed.

The Better Finks stood behind them, each holding an American flag.

Botch and some of the Usual Suspects watched from the sidelines. Mack the Money Man had long since departed with a nice commission, his mission accomplished. Botch couldn't help but feel a swell of pride about what he had pulled off.

Things had gone well. Businesses had made good on their pledge to hit up their employees for donations. Money Man had followed through, making sure everyone had a chance to give. He had managed some good feature stories from the Breeze and local TV stations about the fund raising effort. This was followed by a direct mail campaign and employers asking their people to sign up for payroll deductions.

One of the better stories featured in the Breeze was about the volunteer efforts of the Better Finks, who regularly stood by the barrel in front of the Sons Hotel, ringing bells and encouraging everyone who was heading for the hotel, visitors and Grand Covians alike, to donate to the cause.

The story featured a picture of Andrew Finke waving a flag and ringing a bell. In the background stood Miss Lolita with a big sign that read, "Give Your Fair Square." A person who appeared to be Little Dick stood beside her. Those who knew him thought he looked thin, a little pale but somewhat content.

Yes, Botch thought, things were looking up. And the factory was right on schedule.

******

Mayor Goodenough, flanked by M.P. Booster and Mike Wheelhorse, both of whom had done so much for the fund raising effort, stood beside him for the ribbon cutting ceremony. The mayor didn't care much for this kind of display but had been persuaded that he was needed to commemorate the occasion. He stood poised to snip the red ribbon.

There came a drum roll from the Grand Cove Municipal Band. The Grand Covettes twisted their butts. The mayor read from a brief speech Botch had written for him.

"Grand Covians," he said, speaking into a portable microphone. "I salute you. A few may have questioned our agenda but we're well on our way to making Grand Cove grow. We've got this fine carpet for citizens and visitors alike to walk and drive upon. Our moccasin factory is abuilding. The country is gonna hear about Grand Cove - the city that is gonna grow. And we're doing it the American way."

There were roars of approval up and down Oyster Street. The citizens began reciting the chant they now knew by heart.

> "The city, the city, the city,
> A little bit down a pity,
> For awhile we've been sucking hind titty,
> But this town is gonna grow."

The mayor snipped the ribbon with a big pair of shears. The band and the Grand Covettes stepped out smartly. They were followed by the Better Finks all waving red, white and blue flags. The group began a march down Oyster Street. As they passed by each block the cordons were lowered and citizens fell in behind them, some jumping up and down on the carpet. Sassy and Benny Slax and other merchants stood at attention by their stores. With this many people on hand there were sure to be some shoppers.

Andrew Finke took his time marching along, making sure he put his feet in all the right places. At the beginning and the end of each block there were alternate squares mixed in with the Red carpet.

They were White and Blue. It was, indeed, a Red, White and Blue carpet. Andrew and his Better Fink followers were proud. It was primary colors all the way.

All in all it was a good day for Grand Cove.

Chapter 13   Dedication of the Moccasin Factory

Grand Cove seethed with excitement.

Harry's Moccasin Factory was completed and ready for its grand opening. Thousands of pairs of moccasins had been crafted in preparation for the formal event. The Grand Cove Breeze set the stage with a major story published on Sunday, when it would reach the largest audience, announcing details of the Monday parade and dedication.

DEDICATION SET FOR HARRY'S FACTORY
Citizens will march down Oyster Street
Local holiday declared

*****

Mayor Goodenough had a rare Monday morning meeting on his balcony to get a briefing. He watched the whitecaps lapping against the seawall and in the distance, when he turned his neck left, he could make out the likeness of Harry Moccasin towering over the factory and the Port of Grand Cove.

It was going to be a short meeting, really just a briefing from Botch about the details of the parade. Feather sat with him.

Botch opened the door for himself and joined the mayor and Feather on the balcony.

"We're all set, Mr. Mayor," Botch said.

"The parade will start at 10 a.m. sharp. The Grand Covettes and the Grand Cove Band will lead the parade. Then there will be you and the Usual Suspects - they deserve the notice - with the Citizens falling in line behind. We'll walk on the Carpet to Progress - about two miles - to the dedication site. It's in the parking lot, by Harry's factory," Botch explained.

"Is that what it takes?" the mayor asked a little wearily.

"Absolutely," Botch said. "And the word is already out for everyone in the parade to wear old shoes."

"Old shoes?" Feather asked.

"Yeah," Botch said. "It was a humanitarian thing that our people put together, with Harry's full support. The entrance ticket to the grand opening is the purchase of a chit good for a pair of moccasins. They'll put on their moccasins and throw the old shoes into a truck collecting donations for the Salvation Army. Nothing's too good for those who do good."

******

The crowds began arriving early and were herded into a holding area just off of the south end of Oyster Street. The Grand Covettes and the Grand Grove Band stood in place nearby. The Covettes were decked out in new outfits designed and donated by Sassy as her contribution to the success of the ceremonies.

The Covettes wore white short shorts with the Grand Cove/Open Oyster emblems embroidered on the inner thigh sides of the shorts. Matching tee-shirts bore imprints that read: "Have You Been in Grand Cove?"

A pistol shot pierced the air. The director of the Grand Cove Band, who was standing in front of the parade, made a sharp downswing with his baton.

The Grand Covettes stepped out smartly as the band struck up the tune for a chant written by Lanny Wordsmith - the city's self-proclaimed poet laureate - "We'll Walk Two Miles for Harry."

Mayor Goodenough, the Usual Suspects and the Citizens followed, holding in their hands file card with the words to the chant.

A flatbed truck carrying TV camera crews and reporters and photographers from the Breeze cruised alongside the parade to record the historic occasion. The truck held two big kegs of beer donated by the city's leading beer distributor. They bore a sign that said, "We Got a Case on Harry."

As the parade wended its way down Oyster Street the band struck up the music and the citizens joined in song.

"We'll walk two miles for Harry
We won't dingaling or tarry
We'll walk two miles and be all smiles
For he's our kind of guy."

As the parade neared the Moccasin Factory site everyone could see the likeness of Harry looming in the horizon. As they approached the entrance they could see Harry Himself.

He stood with arms folded at the entrance to the turnstile where the chits were sold. It opened onto the parking lot where festivities and ceremonies would take place. Harry wore a full war bonnet and smiled with his big teeth showing. He stepped out to welcome Mayor Goodenough and the Usual Suspects. "Welcome to Moccasin Factory," he said. "I think we do good."

"We do good, Harry," Botch said.

"Everything seem fine, for now," Harry said.

As the Citizens passed through the turnstile, each paid $30 - men and women , boys and girls - and took their chits to redeem a pair of moccasins that sat, row by row, just inside the entrance, in all kinds of sizes. Harry's crews had worked 16-hour days to make them.

Nearby was a large truck marked "Salvation Army."

In the background were two make-shift stages where bands were playing and off to the right was a huge barbeque pit manned by Stew Tidwell, the city's self-proclaimed barbeque expert. Legend had it Stew could cook anything and make it tasty, including trash fish.

Feather had declined the march but showed up at the dedication site. She watched as Mayor Goodenough and the Usual Suspects passed the turnstile, bought their chits and selected their moccasins. They took off their old shoes and hurled them into the Salvation Army truck.

"I feel good about this," Botch confided to the Mayor as he threw his old shoes into the truck. "We're well on our way to another phase in our goal - Industry - and doing good community work in the process."

"Let's mingle," he added. "This is your great accomplishment."

The mayor and Botch began mingling with the crowd and they ran upon Miss Lolita and Little Dick. She had an arm draped around him and was carrying a sign in support of Harry.

Little Dick didn't look at all like his old self. He was thinner than ever and seemed withdrawn. He was sipping on a beer as Goodenough approached him and put a friendly arm on his shoulder.

"Grand Cove appreciates what you have done," he said.

Little Dick just nodded. Miss Lolita excused herself and in no time returned with two more beers. She handed one to Little Dick and threw a bony arm around him.

"So how are you?" Mayor Goodenough asked Little Dick.

"Ever man has his limits," Little Dick he said. "His limits." He swilled down the beer and held out his paper cup for a refill.

The dueling bands played a drumroll and a quiet fell over the crowd, some still pulling on their moccasins, others stretching their legs or jumping up and down.

Harry Moccasin walked up the steps to the right hand stage and approached a microphone.

He held out his arms. "Harry welcome you. Harry want factory to succeed. First, Grand Cove, then Texas, then the country and the world. Harry want to see a moccasin on every foot. He want Grand Covians to set pace. Buy another pair on way out. Meanwhile, Harry want you to party."

He stepped back from the microphone and held up a beer. The band struck up the tune to, "The City."

The Citizens needed no urging and they began to chant.

> "The city, the city, the city
> A little bit down a pity
> For awhile we've been sucking hind titty
> But this town is gonna grow."

The bands followed up with a new tune which was known as "The Harry Twist." The music was loud and the Citizens excited, helped along by the free beer. Weight challenged Citizens, along with those slim and trim, appeared on the surface of the parking lot which was doubling as a dance floor and began making body motions. On the left stage the Grand Covettes were shaking their butts and their boobs. " The Harry Twist" consisted of nothing more than twisting - butts and guts and boobs. It ended with high kicks. Many moccasins left the feet they were on. Citizens scrambled to find ones that would fit them. There were butts and guts and boobs shaking all over the place.

The bands didn't let up and at one point Harry Moccasin jumped into the middle of it all and began whooping and doing a strange dance. He threw his moccasins into the air. "I buy new pair. You do too," he said. Others filed into a line to eat Stew Tidwell's barbeque. The featured dish was chicken fried mullet and salsa.

"Ain't this great?" Botch said to Mayor Goodenough as he munched on a piece of fish and stifled a gag. "Ain't it great?"

"We'll see," the mayor said as he downed a SBW he had brought along in a flask. "We'll see."

The dancing and the partying were interrupted by a piercing scream. It came from the direction of the barbeque pit. Security guards, hired for the occasion, rushed to the scene, but none knew what to do because they were not trained to do anything.

But they were able to drag Miss Lolita from the edges of the pit. Her hair was singed and ashes were all over her.

"He did it," she gasped as she pointed a bony finger at Little Dick. "He's the one. And all this time I thought....." She passed out while Little Dick just shuffled around.

"What happened?" Botch asked. He was running his hand over his head, over and over again.

Little Dick shot him an acid look. "The factory's open, OK? I've done my civic duty and quite frankly I am through. I'm going to reclaim myself and if necessary I'll shove a moccasin up Harry's ass. I'm going back to suing insurance companies."

"But you seemed so contented," Botch said.

"I fake things," Little Dick said. "After all, I am a lawyer."

Mayor Goodenough draped an arm around Little Dick's shoulder. "Don't worry, son. You done a good job," he said. "And remember the city helps those who help it."

"How?" Little Dick asked. "No pun intended."

"How? You now represent the City as special counsel," the mayor said and patted him again. An EMS unit took Miss Lolita for treatment at the Grand Cove Hospital.

Meanwhile, the bands were playing again and with great fury. The Citizens were dancing with abandon. Sassy and Benny Slax were among them.

As a tune wound down Sissy reached for her left foot and hobbled on her right one.

"What's wrong?" Benny Slax asked.

"I think I've lost my sole," she said. She plopped into a folding chair and massaged her left foot.

""What soul?" Slax joked.

"The sole of my moccasin. It's come off," she said. "Must of been the dancing." She glanced around and noticed some other Citizens were also massaging their feet.

Chapter 14   **Report to the Mayor**

It was Friday afternoon, four days after the Grand Opening of Harry's Moccasin Factory. Mayor Goodenough sat on his balcony, along with Feather, awaiting the arrival of the Usual Suspects for a full report on the dedication. He had already heard some disquieting news - that the soles of lots and lots of moccasins had fallen off during the dedication celebration, and more later. His office had logged a number of complaints from Grand Covians who wanted to know what happened.

He studied his favorite one-legged seagull and wondered where Grand Cove was really headed. He made his own mental inventory: Tourists continued to trickle in; plans to expand the Convention Center were on hold after the fiasco with the Site Committee, but there was, at least, a new industry - the Moccasin Factory, most of which the city had paid for.

He had recently installed a large rear-view mirror on the bayside of the balcony that reflected traffic along Grand Cove Boulevard, which was on the inner-side of City Hall. He wanted to see if traffic flow patterns had been affected by SUVs and over-sized pickups. He watched a herd of them creep from a red light and concluded that, indeed, they were a problem but there was not much he could do about it except bitch to himself until high gasoline prices brought things back into a perspective.

He walked to his wet bar and made another SBW even as he told himself he needed to cut back. He sighed again as he took a pull and wondered briefly what he had gotten himself into. The position of mayor paid only a token sum, but he didn't need the money. What it did carry was the responsibility of the city and its future.

"Where do we go from here?" he asked Feather who sat on the side of the balcony.

"Do the right thing even if it seems wrong," she said.

There was a rapping on the sliding door to the balcony. The mayor opened it and Sassy, Benny Slax, M.P. Booster and the other Usual Suspects poured onto the balcony, including Harry Moccasin.

They all headed for the wet bar, wearing moccasins, and made drinks. Botch walked to the outward side and faced the crowd. He held a tally sheet.

"Mr. Mayor, I am happy to report, very happy to report, that the Grand Opening was great success. Am happy to report that Harry sold more than 20,000 pairs of moccasins that day. A lot of Citizens bought more than one pair. He turned well over half a million bucks."

Harry nodded. "Good but not good enough. Harry want Citizens to buy more."

"What about your plans to expand?" Feather asked. "We thought you were going outside of Grand Cove."

"Harry have to make money here first. Then he expand. He no like to be questioned. Not good idea," he said.

"What about the soles coming off?" she persisted. "There have been complaints."

"Harry make good product. Maybe Citizens expect too much."

"Maybe you need to focus on the quality of your work force - train them well and pay them more," Feather said.

Harry Moccasin frowned. "Harry pays minimum wage. He follow law. No cheat. But no higher."

Sassy held up her hand. "But Mr. Moccasin how are you going sell a product whose soles come off?"

"How do Sassy sell shorts that come off?" Harry countered.

"Only when they're pulled," Sassy said and winked. "Besides, I sell quality stuff."

Harry finished his drink and threw his glass into the bay. "Harry feel insulted."

Booster wedged himself out of his chair and walked to the edge of the balcony and faced the group. He held up both hands, the palms outward.

"Now, let's everyone settle down. We worked hard to get Harry and his factory here and we're not going to lose him,"

Booster said. "I'm proud of the role I had in landing this asset to Grand Cove. Harry's right. We got to show support, give Harry the resources to put more effort into quality control. We got to crawl before we walk," he said and chuckled.

"We've squeezed our folks pretty hard already," Benny Slax said. "They turned all out for the dedication and moccasin buying. Anyone have some thoughts."

"Harry need more," Harry said.

Mike Wheelhorse, who sat off to one side, ran his right hand over this closely-cropped hair. "As all of you know we had pretty good success with the fund raiser for the Carpet. And, I'm still pleased to note, the employees from our refinery area gave their fair squares. Maybe we could build on that theme and get our folks to help Harry a little more."

Botch picked up on it right away. "That's good, Mike. That's good. What about something like this, 'Support Grand Cove. Buy Your Fair Pairs.' We'll work up some brochures and things. This is a concept we can promote," Botch said.

Harry grunted.

Booster, who was still standing at the edge of the balcony, nodded and said, "Let's do it. Let's give it our best shot. We're already in pretty deep." He turned to Mayor Goodenough. "What are your thoughts, Mr. Mayor?"

"You're right about one thing. We're in pretty deep. We do need to hold what we got," Goodenough said. "But here are my thoughts. I think I am simply not going to put up with any more fuckups."

The sternness of his comments got the attention of all of them. Both Botch and Booster appeared to blush slightly.

"You support Harry and Harry make it work," Harry Moccasin said.

"Well, let's get cracking," Botch added. "Let's make it work."

Chapter 15   The Big Blow

Grand Cove Bay was unusually quiet that Friday afternoon in early August. Mayor Goodenough had retired to his balcony for a SBW. The waves of Grand Cove Bay lapped gently against the seawall. He reflected on the past few weeks, since the last meeting of the Usual Suspects. The campaign to get the Citizens to buy more moccasins was having some success and there had been some improvement in the moccasins - so he was told. But his office was still getting complaints. And, as Feather had noted more than once, the Citizens were paying for everything, from the Red Carpet to the moccasins.

He had deliberately stayed out of the way recently, but Botch came by once a week to update him. Goodenough decided he had gone as far as he could. He and the group had set a plan in action and now it would have to play itself out, for good or ill. Botch was his man - he had picked him - and he knew that, too.

It was unusually quiet and he enjoyed it. Feather had been at the ranch for the last three weeks, to, as she had told him, "Get away from this crap." He chided her for swearing and she reminded him who taught her. He chuckled and watched his one-legged seagull take flight. It was a typically warm August day and only a slight breeze blew in, barely ruffling the waters.

******

While the mayor was enjoying the quiet of Grand Cove Bay, a tropical depression had already been building up in the Caribbean Sea, often a spawning ground for tropical storms. But none had so far that year made its way into the Gulf of Mexico, which puts the entire Gulf Coast at potential risk.

In almost no time the tropical depression developed into a storm and lashed the western edge of Cuba with winds of more than 60 miles per hour but not yet a hurricane. But as it moved into the Gulf of Mexico on Saturday it grew in intensity.

Hurricane reconnaissance planes that flew into the storm measured winds of more than 100 miles an hour, well above the 75 mph level used to designate a low-level hurricane. It had become a full-blown hurricane.

As the hurricane moved farther into the Gulf of Mexico, Mayor Goodenough assembled the city's Emergency Disaster Team for routine monitoring. There was little concern that Grand Cove might be in peril.

As the sun set on that beautiful August evening it was aglow and that glow reflected in the clouds.

Benny Slax, Sassy, Pete Garcia and some of the other Usual Suspects were having SBWs at the Sons Hotel to go over things. As they left the entrance to the hotel, which faced to the west, and marveled at the sunset and the reflections in the clouds, Pete said, "You know, there was an old salt in here tonight, a merchant seaman and a friend of mine whose been sailing out of here for years. I walked him out the door-that's the kind of thing I do, of course - and he pointed to that sunset and the reflections. 'It looks like a hurricane sky,' " he told me.

"Not to worry," Sassy said as she bussed him on the cheek. "We're ignored by everyone else. Why would a hurricane be interested."

The hurricane continued to intensify and blow toward the Texas Gulf Coast. By late Saturday hurricane watches had been issued for much of the Texas Gulf Coast, spanning the stretch from Grand Cove on the south to Port Arthur, near the Louisiana border. If the hurricane stayed on course it was projected to move inland somewhere in the middle, well north of Grand Cove.

But early Sunday morning the hurricane moved to the west and became more focused, moving toward the Grand Cove area of the Texas Gulf Coast. Hurricane warnings were issued for the area.

As the storm intensified the barrier islands, already buffeted by winds and high tides, were ordered evacuated.

By late Sunday morning, it became clear that the hurricane was fixed on Grand Cove. The eye, the calm center of a hurricane, had narrowed, making it more powerful.

Thousands of residents boarded up their houses and fled the area, clogging the State Highway and Interstate 37 to San Antonio. Others stayed put, prepared to ride it out. Businesses shut down and boarded up. The American Red Cross began opening shelters.

Mayor Goodenough and the Emergency Disaster Team set up headquarters in the basement of the Grand Cove Police Headquarters, a sturdy red-brick building. His team was in touch with the Governor's office to ask for National Guard help should that become necessary. He and his staff went over plans for a curfew.

Red and black flags, already beginning to shred, whipped in the wind from a pole in the Grand Cove Marina signaling their warning: HURRICANE!

******

The news media love a hurricane and when it became apparent that Grand Cove would likely feel the brunt of the powerful storm, they descended upon Grand Cove from various points they had been monitoring along the Gulf Coast. Grand Cove Boulevard soon bustled with satellite trucks and broadcast journalists, newspaper reporters and photographers.

Broadcasters vied for street light poles and sturdy palm trees along Grand Cove Boulevard so they could wrap themselves around them as they broadcast reports of the impending strike, their hair blowing in the wind and the rain beating against them.

"Officials are preparing for the worst," one shouted into his microphone, his right arm hugging a palm tree. "The city could be wiped off the map."

At long last Grand Cove, which had so sought some publicity, was getting noticed. As the hurricane came closer the media headed in a herd to the Sons Hotel. There they began knocking down SBWs while watching briefly from the balcony of the hotel and then retiring to the more secure Deal Room to ride it out.

******

The first half of the hurricane blew in from the north - the western edge of the swirl. It was like a giant rake that moved in an arc across the city. Structures in the path of the prongs were raked away while those in between were left wet but largely unscathed.

The northerly direction of the winds pushed the waters of Grand Cove Bay outward. Hulls of boats still moored in the Marina briefly scraped the bottom of the bay.

Then the winds swung around, blowing in from the south-southwest, bringing with them torrential rains as the hurricane continued with its one-two punch to the city, blowing not with malice but with complete indifference. Grand Cove just happened to be in its way.

Roofs were ripped from houses, trailer parks leveled, windows blown from office buildings, hurling shards in all directions. Trees were uprooted, including some of the stately palms that lined Grand Cove Boulevard. Cars were overturned, their windows and windshields smashed. Fences were blown down, including the large one erected near Grand Cove Airport to shield the shotgun houses and garbage pit from the view of visitors. The monument to Harry Moccasin lay face down in the waters of the Port of Grand Cove. The roof of the factory was blown away and two of the flimsy walls collapsed. Moccasins, in various stages of completion, were strewn all about, mixed in with squares of the Carpet from Oyster Street, which was ruined.

Power was knocked out and telephone lines down. Grand Cove was devastated and alone. No part of the city was left untouched, including the posh homes along Grand Cove Boulevard.

After a furious four-hour blow, the hurricane moved inland and began to slowly blow itself out.

The following morning the sun peeped out briefly and people ventured out to see what was left of their city while those who had evacuated awaited word on when they would be allowed to return.

National Guardsmen, who had moved in during the night, patroled the streets. State and federal officials began arriving to inspect the damage, promise assistance and pose for pictures.

******

Weather experts termed it one of the most powerful hurricanes of record. The gauge at Grand Cove Airport clocked winds of 160 miles an hour before it was blown down and its readings fixed. A special supplement to the Grand Cove Breeze, published a week later, included a photograph of a stout telephone pole split by the blunt end of a length of lumber that had been forced through it by the powerful winds. The hurricane had blown in quickly. It all happened so fast a lot of people never got its name.

Chapter 16   **Report From the Mayor**

Grand Cove Bay was calm once again although the city was still in the midst of trying to recover. The curfew had been lifted, the National Guardsmen gone and most power and telephone service restored. But a lot of rebuilding remained to be done and decisions to be made.

Mayor Goodenough sat on his balcony, sipping a double SBW. It had been a week since the hurricane passed through. He had been busy meeting with federal and state officials and working with his staff to restore a semblance of order and direction. Many people remained homeless and the damage was great.

The Usual Suspects had been asking for a meeting although events were now out of their hands. He was awaiting them as well as Harry Moccasin who was asked to attend.

Feather had returned from the ranch and been assigned the task of preparing a status report.

Mayor Goodenough was more pensive than usual as he watched the calm waters of Grand Cove Bay lap gently against the seawall while behind him the city still lay in disrepair. Why Grand Cove? he asked himself. He had no answer.

There was a rapping at the door to the balcony. "They're here," Feather said as she slid open the door. The Usual Suspects, along with Harry Moccasin, converged on the balcony and rushed to the bar to make themselves double SBWs. All were talking at once.

Mayor Goodenough gave them time to make their drinks and get settled.

He strode to the outward end of the balcony after they were assembled, some seated, others standing, because the group was larger than usual. He turned with his back against the railing and faced them. He held in his hands the report that Feather had prepared.

"Thanks for coming," he said. "As you know its been a little windy here lately." He attempted a chuckle.

He glanced over the report. "I wanted to bring you up to date. There's bad news and some good news. We were lucky in that no one in Grand Cove lost his life as a direct result of the hurricane but some in the area did. A lot of people got hurt from such things as falling roofs and flying glass. The hospitals reported four deaths from heart attacks but whether they were hurricane related or not we just don't know. Probably were." He paused to take a sip of his SBW.

"We've sustained a lot of damage. The insurance people say the damage to the city and area will be more than a hundred million but we don't have a real good handle on it yet. It could be higher. The Carpet is ruined and what remains of it is being scraped off by dozers. The airport had some damage but is back in business. Most of the roof of the Convention Center was blown away. A lot of houses were damaged, some destroyed, so we have a homeless problem. The Red Cross shelters are still open for them and the feds have promised they'll have mobile homes rolling in soon.

"The feds are also sending other folks and equipment to help our people clear away the debris - downed trees and the like," he continued. "And, as you know, Harry's Moccasin Factory was destroyed."

Harry Moccasin grunted as if to acknowledge his loss.

The mayor continued with his report. "On a more positive note, insurance adjusters are all over the city and being generous with their damage assessments. There's going to be a lot of money flowing into the city. The city itself also stands to gain some money from damage to places like the old Convention Center. The auto repair shops are at capacity, fixing dents and replacing windows and windshields. Construction crews are pouring into the city to fix roofs, repair houses and businesses and rebuild fences."

He paused and took another sip of his SWB . He glanced again at the report Feather had prepared. "Course, not all of these folks can be trusted but a lot can. I've been telling our Citizens to check'em out before signing a contract."

Botch sat near the bar, rubbing his hands.

The mayor nodded toward Pete Garcia. "How'd you come out, Pete?"

"Amazing well," he said. "The Sons is a solid piece of work. We lost some windows and a bit of roof but we're back in business and filled to the brim. All these folks coming into the city on business have got to stay somewhere and a lot of them are staying with me. In fact, since business is good and I'll have a little insurance money to play with I am considering an expansion. Maybe add a small tower with more rooms and expand my modest convention space. Some of the folks here to help rebuild may just come back to visit."

There was applause from around the balcony.

"You're a good one, Pete," Sassy said.

Botch raised his hand and arose. "Mr. Mayor, with all of this money flowing in we got a chance to really rebuild. We can relay that carpet and build new fences by the airport and help Harry get back in business. We can promote this puppy as the city that is not only growing but remaking itself."

The mayor said nothing.

After Botch sat down the mayor nodded toward Harry Moccasin. "Well, Chief," he said, "we got a chance to redo that factory and maybe make it better. What do you think?"

Harry Moccasin arose and briefly glanced down at his feet. "Harry been thinking things over. He decided he no rebuild. He go offshore with project. That is trend, you know, and Harry like to keep up. And help cheaper."

M.P. Booster, who considered the moccasin factory his big win for the city, worked himself out of his chair and stood, red in the face. "Harry go offshore! We work hard to get Harry here. City do lot for Harry."

"Harry take insurance money and run. No like hurricanes. He go offshore," Harry Moccasin repeated.

Feather stood. "I think you've made a good decision," she said quietly. "Why don't you take your crap and leave. Certainly you won't find any hurricanes offshore."

There were gasps from some of the Usual Suspects.

Harry Moccasin began stomping on the balcony and let out a war whoop. "Take crap and leave. Take crap and leave," he shouted. "You bet he take crap and leave. Take money and run. Consider it revenge of the Indians."

He stomped again and fixed his gaze on Feather. "Harry never like you. You as much a bitch as hurricane."

Feather sat down and smiled. "Was it a she?" she asked.

Mayor Goodenough strode to where Harry Moccasin was standing. "Take it easy, Harry. Take it easy," he said, looking Harry Moccasin straight in the eyes. "But taking all things into account I think you've made the right decision."

"And you'll be leaving tonight. We'll see that you get a ride to the airport. You can straighten out your affairs from offshore, whereever that is," the mayor said.

Harry Moccasin, taken aback by the blunt statement, sat down.

"Well," the mayor continued. "That's about it. I'll keep all of you posted. Now let's get about rebuilding our city."

The Usual Suspects began to leave, none with much to say.

"Hang around for a minute, Botch," the mayor said. "We need to talk."

Botch headed for the bar and made himself another drink. "Whatever you say, chief," he said and blushed when he realized he had used the wrong title.

The two of them were alone on the balcony. Mayor Goodenough looked at him with a bit of sadness but resolve. "Botch," he said, "you did what we asked of you. I got no complaints. It just didn't work out so we're gonna try to put Grand Cove on a new path - more substance than hype. We got a chance now. We'll give you some going away money but our project is over."

" I understand," Botch said. "We gave it a good shot."

"That we did," the mayor said. "That we did. And learned a lot in the process. What will you do with yourself?"

"I'll be fine," Botch said. "Think I'll head up to Austin and see if I can help some of those high-tech companies with a little promotion. Some of the dot.coms need help."

"After you get set up keep us in mind," the mayor said.

"I kinda figured Harry would pull out on us or continue with a piece of crap so that is why I said what I did," the mayor continued. "I been thinking about using the factory grounds as a site for a tech training center, a place where our kids can learn the new technology and maybe attract a firm or two. Something that pays better than moccasin wages. I've talked with some of the education folks here and they think it is 'doable', as they put it."

"I'll stay in touch," Botch said. "You're okay."

They shook hands and had another drink, just between the two of them.

******

There was an incessant ringing from the mayor's inner office as he and Botch finished their drinks. The mayor finally pushed a button that transferred the call to his balcony.

"Who? Speak up man. I can barely hear you," the mayor said into the phone. He listened for a few more seconds and took a sip of his SBW.

"Yes, I remember you," the mayor said. "Yessir, I really do."

"Your timing is good," the mayor added. "Standby. Mr. Botsford is right here."

The mayor handed the phone to Botch.

Botch listened for a full two minutes. "That's wonderful, Huey," he said. "Glad you carried through on your promise. Yes. The hurricane was a bad one but the city is going to rebuild. By the way, I'll be leaving Grand Cove but if there is ever any serious interest in a convention the main men can get in touch with the mayor's office or with Pete Garcia at the Sons Hotel.

103

You remember it, I assume. And I hope you get better." He hung up the phone.

Botch turned to the mayor. "That was the guy with the Site Committee who took us for a kind of ride. Said he had put in a good word for us. I made him promise before he left that he'd do that. I think I mentioned it."

"I recall," the mayor said. "Where was he calling from?"

"From his house," Botch said. "He had a little trouble speaking. Said he's still kind of recovering from a jaw problem." He looked down at his feet, a little embarrassed. "Peewee, eh, Sergeant Ratlidge, took'em to the airport the morning they left Grand Cove. Kind of insurance."

"Maybe something good will happen after all," Botch added. "At least we're on the map."

"Time for another drink?" the mayor asked.

"You better believe it," Botch said as he strode to the bar and poured one for each of them. He took a sip. "I'm gonna miss this bay water," he said.

The mayor nodded. Both seemed a little reluctant to end it just on the quality of a drink of scotch made with bay water.

Botch cleared his throat. "Mr. Mayor, may I presume for a minute?"

"You may," he said.

"Well, I was just wondering about something. I agree that Harry Moccasin is an ass but we had to stroke him. And I know that you care a lot for Feather and value her opinion. She's a sharp one," Botch said.

"I do know that," the mayor said. "Yessir, I do." He glanced out over the tranquil bay.

"So do I," Botch said. "And I've come to really respect her. She's got a lot of class and insight." He seemed a little agitated. "So why did you let that fake Indian get away with insulting her? Right here in front of the Usual Suspects, our own people."

"I appreciate your interest and sentiments," the mayor said. "But Feather is a tough one. She can deal with it. And I am not a man of violence."

He glanced out over the bay once again and spotted his one-legged seagull. He studied it for a moment and turned back to face Botch. A hint of a grin played at his lips.

"Guess who's driving Harry Moccasin to the airport tonight," the mayor said.

About the Author

Jim Wood is a veteran reporter who toiled in the newspaper vineyards for more than three decades, reporting for the Corpus Christi Caller-Times and San Antonio Express-News. He retired a few years back to devote more time to other writing pursuits. He is the author of numerous freelance articles.

Much of his work as a reporter dealt with urban affairs, giving him first hand knowledge of issues facing the nation's cities and how they are trying to address them. While many cities have goals similar to those of Grand Cove, Wood says he never met any leaders quite like those of Grand Cove, a fictional city.

He currently lives in San Antonio.

www.ingramcontent.com/pod-product-compliance
Lightning Source LLC
Chambersburg PA
CBHW030339290526
45785CB00004B/1530